American Drama from Its Beginnings to the Present

compiled by

E. Hudson Long

Baylor University

APPLETON-CENTURY-CROFTS

Educational Division

New York **MEREDITH CORPORATION**

Preface

THE FOLLOWING BIBLIOGRAPHY is intended for graduate and advanced undergraduate students in courses on the American drama and related subjects who desire a convenient guide to scholarship in the field. The listing is necessarily selective, but every effort has been made to provide ample coverage of the major works and topics, with emphasis on work published in the twentieth century.

In order to keep this bibliography to a practical size, it has been necessary to omit a number of references: unpublished dissertations, literary histories (except for a very few), short notes and explications (except when they contain important data).

In general, the compiler has attempted to steer a middle course between the brief lists of references included in the average textbook and the long professional bibliography in which significant items are often lost in the sheer number of references given. This bibliography should materially assist the student in his effort to survey a topic, write reports and term papers, prepare for examinations, and do independent reading. Attention is called to four features intended to enhance its utility.

(1) Extra margin on each page permits listing of library call numbers of often-used items.

(2) Space at the bottom of every page permits inclusion of additional entries, and blank pages for notes follow the final entry.

(3) An index by author follows the bibliography proper.

(4) The Index and cross-reference numbers direct the reader to the page and position-on-the-page of the desired entry. Thus, in an entry such as

Quinn, Arthur H. "Eugene O'Neill." See 45.18.

v

the number 45.18 indicates that the entry referred to is on page 45, and is the 18th item on that page. Both page numbers and individual entry numbers are conspicuous in size and position so that the process of finding entries is fast as well as simple.

An asterisk following an entry indicates a work of "special importance" in the field. Other annotations, given in brackets, which may conclude an entry are: abbreviations of paperback publishers and series numbers, all based on the list of abbreviations given in *Paperbound Books in Print*; a phrase describing the subject of an allusive title.

Symbols identifying journals follow the forms given in the Table of Symbols at the beginning of the annual *PMLA* bibliography. The symbols and their meanings are as follows:

ABC	American Book Collector
AH	American Heritage
AI	American Imago
AL	American Literature
Am Hist Rev	American Historical Review
Am Mercury	American Mercury
AQ	American Quarterly
AR	Antioch Review
ArQ	Arizona Quarterly
AS	American Speech
ASch	American Scholar
BB	Bulletin of Bibliography
BNYPL	Bulletin of the New York Public Library
Bucknell U Stud	Bucknell University Studies
BuR	Bucknell Review
CathW	Catholic World
CE	College English
CJ	Classical Journal
CLAJ	College Language Association Journal
CLC	Columbia Library Columns
ColM	Colorado Magazine
ColQ	Colorado Quarterly
CritQ	Critical Quarterly
Cweal	Commonweal
DR	Dalhousie Review
DramS	Drama Survey
EA	Etudes Anglaises
EIC	Essays in Criticism (Oxford)
EJ	English Journal
ELN	English Language Notes
ES	English Studies
Essex Inst Hist Coll	Essex Institute Historical Collections

ETJ	Educational Theatre Journal
EUQ	Emory University Quarterly
FR	French Review
GaR	Georgia Review
GHQ	Georgia Historical Quarterly
GQ	German Quarterly
HudR	Hudson Review
Ind Mag Hist	Indiana Magazine of History
JA	Jarbuch für Amerikastudien
JAAC	Journal of Aesthetics and Art Criticism
JEGP	Journal of English and Germanic Philology
KHQ	Kansas Historical Quarterly
KR	Kenyon Review
La Hist Quart	Louisiana Historical Quarterly
LCUP	Library Chronicle of University of Pennsylvania
LJ	Library Journal
LSUSHS	Louisiana State University Studies, Humanities Series
MAQR	Michigan Alumni Quarterly Review
MD	Modern Drama
MHM	Maryland Historical Magazine
MichH	Michigan History
Missi Valley Hist Rev	Mississippi Valley Historical Review
MLN	Modern Language Notes
MLQ	Modern Language Quarterly
MQR	Michigan Quarterly Review
NCHR	North Carolina Historical Review
NDQ	North Dakota Quarterly
NEQ	New England Quarterly
NJHSP	New Jersey Historical Society Proceedings
NL	Nouvelles Littéraires
NMQ	New Mexico Quarterly
North Am Rev	North American Review
NOQ	Northwest Ohio Quarterly
N&Q	Notes and Queries
NY	New Yorker
NYFQ	New York Folklore Quarterly
NYTBR	New York Times Book Review
NY Times Mag	New York Times Magazine
PAAS	Proceedings, American Antiquarian Society
PBSA	Papers of the Bibliographical Society of America
PMLA	Publications of the Modern Language Association of America
PR	Partisan Review
Princeton Alumni Wk	Princeton Alumni Weekly
PrS	Prairie Schooner
QJS	Quarterly Journal of Speech
QQ	Queen's Quarterly
RIH	Rhode Island History
SatR	Saturday Review

SAQ	South Atlantic Quarterly
Shakespeare Assn Bul	Shakespeare Association Bulletin
SHQ	Southwestern Historical Quarterly
SoR	Southern Review
SP	Studies in Philology
SR	Sewanee Review
SRL	Saturday Review of Literature
SS	Scandinavian Studies and Notes
SWR	Southwest Review
Sym	Symposium
TA	Theatre Annual
TamR	Tamarack Review
TArts	Theatre Arts
TC	Twentieth Century
TCL	Twentieth Century Literature
TDR	Tulane Drama Review
TSE	Tulane Studies in English
TSLL	Texas Studies in Literature and Language
UKCR	University of Kansas City Review
U Penn Lib Chron	University of Pennsylvania Library Chronicle
UTQ	University of Toronto Quarterly
U Wichita Bul	University of Wichita Bulletin
VMHB	Virginia Magazine of History and Biography
VQR	Virginia Quarterly Review
VtQ	Vermont Quarterly
WASAL	Wisconsin Academy of Science and Letters
WF	Western Folklore
WHR	Western Humanities Review
WMQ	William and Mary Quarterly
WSCL	Wisconsin Studies in Contemporary Literature
WR	Western Review
XUS	Xavier University Studies
Yale U Lib Gaz	Yale University Library Gazette
YR	Yale Review

Note: *The publisher and compiler invite suggestions for additions to future editions of the bibliography.*

Contents

Reference Works

1 CHAPMAN, John. *The Burns Mantle Best Plays of 1947–1948.* New York: Dodd, Mead, 1948. (Subsequent annual volumes thereafter giving a record of the season and synopses of plays.)

2 *A Guide to the Study of the United States of America.* Prepared by Roy P. Basler, Donald H. Mugridge, and Blanche P. McCrum. Washington, D.C.: Library of Congress, 1960. (Useful short sketches.)

3 HART, James D. *The Oxford Companion to American Literature.* 4th ed. New York: Oxford UP, 1965. (Especially helpful for brief biographies.)

4 HARTNOLL, Phyllis, ed. *The Oxford Companion to the Theatre.* Rev. ed. London: Oxford UP, 1967. (A standard reference work that includes the American theatre.)

5 LOVELL, John, Jr. *Digests of Great American Plays: Complete Summaries of More Than 100 Plays from the Beginnings to the Present.* New York: Crowell, 1961. (Summaries by acts with useful indexes to authors and actors.)

6 MANTLE, Burns. *The Best Plays of 1919–1920.* New York: Dodd, Mead, 1920. (Beginning in 1920 a volume has appeared for each year, giving a record of the season and synopses of the best plays. The series is now edited by John Chapman.)

7 RIGDON, Walter. *The Biographical Encyclopaedia & Who's Who of the American Theatre.* New York: Heineman, 1966. (Comprehensive reference guide.)*

8 SOBEL, Bernard. *Theatre Handbook and Digest of Plays.* New York: Crown, 1940.

9 THRALL, W. F., and Addison HIBBARD. *A Handbook to Literature.* Rev. and enlarged by C. Hugh Holman. New York: Odyssey, 1960. [Ody.] (A fine, compact, and comprehensive reference work. Very helpful for defining literary terms.)

American Literary History

10 BROOKS, Van Wyck. *Makers and Finders: A History of the Writers in America, 1800–1915.* New York: Dutton, 1936–1952. (Artistic treatment of the literary life of the times.) Includes: *The Flowering of New England, 1815–1865* (1936). [D3-Duttn.] *New England Indian Summer, 1865–1915* (1940). [D164-Duttn.] *The World of Washington Irving* (1944). *The Times of Melville and Whitman* (1947). *The Confident Years: 1885–1915* (1952).

11 COMMAGER, Henry Steele. *The American Mind: An Interpretation of American Thought and Character Since the 1880's.* New Haven, Conn.: Yale UP, 1950. [Y7-Yale.]

12 HORTON, Rod. W., and Herbert W. EDWARDS. *Backgrounds of American Literary Thought.* New York: Appleton-Century-Crofts, 1952. [Appl.] (Helpful for social, economic, and philosophical trends.)

1   HOWARD, Leon. *Literature and the American Tradition*. Garden City, N.Y.: Doubleday, 1960. [A329-Anch.]

2   MORRIS, Lloyd. *Postscript to Yesterday*. New York: Random, 1947. (Treats the authors from 1895 to 1945 as part of the social scene.)

3   PARRINGTON, Vernon Louis. *Main Currents in American Thought*. 3 vols. New York: Harcourt, Brace, 1927. [Vol. I, HB4-Harv.; Vol. II, HB5-Harv.] (A standard work.)

4   QUINN, Arthur Hobson, ed. *The Literature of the American People*. New York: Appleton-Century-Crofts, 1951. (Excellent sections by Kenneth B. Murdock, A. H. Quinn, Clarence Gohdes, George F. Whicher.)*

5   SPILLER, Robert E. *The Cycle of American Literature: An Essay in Historical Criticism*. New York: Macmillan, 1956. [MT643-Ment.] (Brief, general treatment.)

6   SPILLER, Robert E., et al., eds. *Literary History of the United States*. Rev. ed. New York: Macmillan, 1953. (Extensive treatment by a number of eminent scholars.)*

7   TAYLOR, Walter F. *The Story of American Letters*. Chicago: Regnery, 1956. (A revision of *A History of American Letters* [1936].)

8   THORP, Willard. *American Writing in the Twentieth Century*. Cambridge: Harvard UP, 1960.

9   TRENT, William P., et al., eds. *The Cambridge History of American Literature*. 3 vols. New York: Macmillan, 1917. (Still interesting for comparative criticism.)

Bibliographies of the American Drama

10 *American Literature*. Periodical, published quarterly since 1929 by the Duke Univ. Press, Durham, N.C. (Each issue contains a listing of articles on American literature appearing in current periodicals, prepared by the Bibliography Committee of the American Literature Section of the Modern Language Association.)*

11 BAKER, Blanche M. *Dramatic Bibliography. An Annotated List of Books on the History and Criticism of the Drama and Stage and on the Allied Arts of the Theatre*. New York: Wilson, 1933.

12 BAKER, Blanche M. *The Theatre and Allied Arts: A Guide to Books Dealing with the History, Criticism, and Technic of the Drama, and Theatre and Related Arts and Crafts*. New York: Wilson, 1952. (Basic reference work.)*

13 BERGQUIST, G. William, ed. *Three Centuries of English and American Plays*. New York and London: Hafner, 1963. (A valuable checklist of American plays, 1714–1830.)

14 BLANCK, Jacob. *Bibliography of American Literature*. 10 vols. New Haven: Yale UP, 1955– . (In progress.)*

15 CORNYN, Stan. *A Selective Index to Theatre Magazine*. New York: Scarecrow, 1964. (Covers 1900–1930.)

1   *Dramatic Compositions Copyrighted in the United States, 1870–* . (Published annually by the Copyright Office, Library of Congress, Washington, D.C.)

2   GILDER, Rosamund, and George FREEDLEY. *Theatre Collections in Libraries and Museums.* New York: Theatre Arts, 1936.

3   GOHDES, Clarence. *Literature and Theater of the States and Regions of the U.S.A.: An Historical Bibliography.* Durham, N.C.: Duke UP, 1967.

4   HILL, Frank P. *American Plays Printed, 1714–1830.* Stanford U, Cal.: Stanford UP, 1934. (Includes 335 plays.)

5   LEARY, Lewis G. *Articles on American Literature, 1900–1950.* Durham, N.C.: Duke UP, 1954. (A supplementary volume is in preparation by Leary and Daniel W. Patterson.)

6   LUDWIG, Richard M. "Bibliography Supplement." *Literary History of the United States.* Ed. by Robert E. Spiller, et al. New York: Macmillan, 1959.

7   *MLA International Bibliography*, under various eds. Published each May as a supplement to *PMLA.* (Lists scholarly and critical works of the preceding year.)

8   OTTEMILLER, John H. *Index to Plays in Collections.* Washington, D.C.: Scarecrow P, 1951. (Index of all published anthologies to 1950.)

9   SANTANIELLO, A. E. *Theatre Books in Print.* 2d ed. New York: Drama Book Shop, 1966. (A useful compilation.)

10 SPILLER, Robert E., et al. *Literary History of the United States.* Vol. III. New York: Macmillan, 1948. (Indispensable.)*

11 STRATMAN, Carl J. *Bibliography of the American Theatre: Excluding New York City.* Chicago: Loyola UP, 1965. (Lists publications on theatrical activities of all kinds.)

12 WEINGARTER, Joseph A. *Modern American Playwrights, 1918–1948: A Bibliography.* New York: Privately Printed, 1948.

13 WOODRESS, James, ed. *American Literary Scholarship: An Annual/1963.* Durham, N.C.: Duke UP, 1965, and annually since. (Each volume has a section on American drama.)*

Anthologies of the American Drama

14 *America's Lost Plays.* 10 vols. Bloomington, Ind.: Indiana UP, 1965. (A reprinting in ten double-volumes of plays originally published by the Princeton UP under the general editorship of Barrett H. Clark.)*

15 BAKER, George Pierce, ed. *Modern American Plays.* New York: Harcourt, Brace & Howe, 1920.

1 BENTLEY, Eric, ed. *From the American Drama*. Garden City, N.Y.: Doubleday, 1956. [A48D-Doubl.] (Contains five plays.)

2 CASSIDY, Frederic G., ed. *Modern American Plays*. New York: Longmans, Green, 1949. (Only six plays.)

3 CERF, Bennett, ed. *The Pocket Book of Modern American Plays*. New York: Pocket Books, 1942. (Only four plays.)

4 CERF, Bennett, and Van H. CARTMELL, eds. *Sixteen Famous American Plays*. Introduction by Brooks Atkinson. Garden City, N.Y.: Garden City Pub., 1941. (A good collection.)

5 CERF, Bennett, and Van H. CARTMELL, eds. *S.R.O.: The Most Successful Plays in the History of the American Stage*. Garden City, N.Y.: Doubleday Doran, 1944. (From *Uncle Tom's Cabin* to *Life With Father*.)

6 CLARK, Barrett H., ed. *Favorite American Plays of the Nineteenth Century*. Princeton, N.J.: Princeton UP, 1943. (Contains ten plays.)

7 CLARK, Barrett H., and William H. DAVENPORT, eds. *Nine Modern American Plays*. New York: Appleton-Century-Crofts, 1951.

8 CLURMAN, Harold, ed. *Famous American Plays of the 1930s*. New York: Dell, 1959. [2478-LE, Dell.]

9 COE, Kathryn, and William H. CORDELL, eds. *The Pulitzer Prize Plays*. New York: Random, 1940. (Twenty prize plays.)*

10 CORDELL, Richard A., ed. *Twentieth Century Plays, American: Eight Representative Selections*. New York: Ronald, 1947.

11 *The Critics' Prize Plays*. Introduction by George Jean Nathan. Cleveland: World, 1945.

12 DOWNER, Alan S., ed. *American Drama*. New York: Crowell, 1960. [TY-Crow.] (Six plays from Tyler to Williams.)

13 GASSNER, John, ed. *Best American Plays*. New York: Crown, 1939–1963. (An important series that covers the American drama from 1916 to 1963.) It includes: *Twenty-five Best Plays of the Modern American Theatre, Early Series* (1949). *Twenty Best Plays of the Modern American Theatre* (1939). *Best Plays of the Modern American Theatre: Second Series* (1947). *Best American Plays: Third Series* (1952). *Best American Plays: Fourth Series* (1958). *Best American Plays, Fifth Series* (1963). *Best American Plays, Supplementary Volume* (1961).*

14 GAVER, Jack, ed. *Critics' Choice: New York Drama Critics' Circle Prize Plays, 1935–55*. New York: Hawthorn, 1955. (Important collection.)*

15 HALLINE, Allan G., ed. *American Plays*. New York: American Book, 1935. (From the beginning to 1935.)

16 HALLINE, Allan G., ed. *Six Modern American Plays*. New York: Modern Library, 1951. [T85-Mod. Lib.]

1   HATCHER, Harlan, ed. *Modern American Dramas*. New York: Harcourt, Brace, 1949.

2   HEWES, Henry, ed. *Famous American Plays of the 1940s*. New York: Dell, 1960. [2490-LE, Dell.]

3   HILDRETH, William H., and Wilson R. DUMBLE, eds. *Five Contemporary American Plays*. New York: Harper, 1939.

4   MACGOWAN, Kenneth, ed. *Famous American Plays of the 1920s*. New York: Dell, 1960.

5   MAYORGA, Margaret, ed. *The Best One-Act Plays of 1946–1947*. New York: Dodd, Mead, 1947.

6   MILLER, Jordan Y., ed. *American Dramatic Literature: Ten Modern Plays in Historical Perspective*. New York: McGraw-Hill, 1961.

7   MOODY, Richard, ed. *Dramas from the American Theatre 1762–1909*. New York: World, 1966. (A representative anthology from Francis Hopkinson to Clyde Fitch with well-selected bibliographies.)

8   MOSES, Montrose J., ed. *Dramas of Modernism and Their Forerunners*. Boston: Little, Brown, 1941.

9   MOSES, Montrose J., ed. *Representative American Dramas, National and Local*. Boston: Little, Brown, 1925. (Covers the period 1894–1924.)

10 MOSES, Montrose J., ed. *Respresentative Plays by American Dramatists*. 3 vols. New York: Benjamin Bloom, 1964. (A reissue of the 1918 publication. Volume one covers the period from 1765 to 1819; volume two from 1815 to 1858; volume three from 1856 to 1917. An indispensable collection with historical and critical introductions.)*

11 MOSES, Montrose J., and Joseph W. KRUTCH, eds. *Representative American Dramas*. Boston: Heath, 1941. (Fine collection of twenty-two plays from 1894 to 1937.)*

12 *New Voices in the American Theatre*. Foreword by Brooks Atkinson. New York: Modern Library, 1955. (Contains six plays.)

13 QUINN, Arthur Hobson, ed. *Contemporary American Plays*. New York: Scribner's, 1923.

14 QUINN, Arthur Hobson, ed. *Representative American Plays*. 7th ed. New York: Appleton-Century-Crofts, 1953. (A complete survey with authentic texts. Indispensable.)*

15 *The Theatre Guild Anthology*. New York: Random, 1936.

Histories of the American Drama

16 MAYORGA, Margaret G. *A Short History of the American Drama*. New York: Dodd, Mead, 1932. (Brief treatment, but useful.)

17 MESERVE, Walter J. *An Outline History of American Drama*. Totowa, N.J.: Littlefield, Adams, 1965. [68-Littlef.] (A useful and sensible guide.)

1   MOSES, Montrose J. *The American Dramatist*. New York: Benjamin Blom, 1964. (A reissue of an important study first published in 1925.)*

2   QUINN, Arthur Hobson. *A History of the American Drama from the Beginning to the Civil War*. Rev. ed. New York: Crofts, 1944. (The standard history of the period.)*

3   QUINN, Arthur Hobson. *A History of the American Drama from the Civil War to the Present Day*. Rev. ed. New York: Crofts, 1937. (The standard history through 1935.)*

Histories of the American Theatre

4   ANDERSON, John. *The American Theatre*. New York: Dial, 1938.

5   BLUM, Daniel C. *A Pictorial History of the American Theatre, 1900–1950*. New York: Greenberg, 1950. (Fifty years of the theatre in pictures, scant text.)

6   CRAWFORD, Mary Caroline. *The Romance of the American Theatre*. Boston: Little, Brown, 1913. (Informal study of trends, especially the nineteenth century.)

7   HORNBLOW, Arthur. *A History of the Theatre in America*. 2 vols. Philadelphia: Lippincott, 1919. (More about the theatre than the drama.)

8   HUGHES, Glenn. *A History of the American Theatre, 1700–1950*. New York: French, 1951. (Indispensable.)*

9   MOREHOUSE, Ward. *Matinee Tomorrow*. New York: McGraw-Hill, 1949. (The American stage from 1898 to 1948.)

10 MORRIS, Lloyd. *Curtain Time*. New York: Random, 1953. (Informal account of the American theatre from 1820 to 1952.)

11 ODELL, George C. D. *Annals of the New York Stage*. 15 vols. New York: Columbia UP, 1949. (A great work of extensive scope by an industrious scholar.)*

12 TAUBMAN, Howard. *The Making of the American Theatre*. New York: Coward McCann, 1965. (Astute evaluation of stage presentations from the beginning to the present.)

Accounts of Actors and Producers

13 BINNS, Archie. *Mrs. Fiske and the American Theatre*. New York: Crown, 1955.

14 BLUM, Daniel C. *Great Stars of the American Stage*. New York: Greenberg, 1952. (Pictures, little text.)

15 DOWNER, Alan S., ed. *The Memoir of John Durang, American Actor, 1785–1816*. Pittsburgh: U of Pittsburgh P, 1966.

1 DUNLAP, William. *Diary of William Dunlap.* (New York Historical Society Collections. Vols. 62–64.) New York: New York Historical Society, 1930.

2 FROHMAN, Daniel. *Memories of a Manager.* New York: Doubleday, 1911.

3 HAYES, Helen, with Sandford DOBY. *On Reflection.* Philadelphia: M. Evans, 1968.

4 JEFFERSON, Joseph. *The Autobiography of Joseph Jefferson.* New York: Century, 1890.*

5 KNEPLER, Henry. *The Gilded Stage: The Years of the Great International Actresses.* New York: Morrow, 1968.

6 MATHEWS, Anne Jackson. *Memories of Charles Mathews, Comedian.* London: Bentley, 1838. (Good account of the early nineteenth-century American theatre.)

7 MOODY, Richard. *Edwin Forrest.* New York: Knopf, 1960. (Scholarly account of America's first great actor.)*

8 MOSES, Montrose J. *The Fabulous Forrest.* Boston: Little, Brown, 1929.

9 MOSES, Montrose J. *Famous Actor-Families in America.* New York: Crowell, 1906.

10 MOWATT, Anna Cora. *The Autobiography of an Actress.* Boston: Ticknor, Reed, and Fields, 1854.

11 RUGGLES, Eleanor. *Prince of Players.* New York: Norton, 1953. (Biography of Edwin Booth.)

12 SKINNER, Cornelia Otis. *Family Circle.* Boston: Houghton Mifflin, 1943.

13 SKINNER, Otis. *Footlights and Spotlights.* Indianapolis, Ind.: Bobbs, Merrill, 1924.

14 SMITH, Solomon F. *Theatrical Management in the West and South for Thirty Years.* New York: Harper, 1868.

15 WALLACK, Lester. *Memories of Fifty Years.* New York: Scribner's, 1889.

16 WEMYSS, F. C. *Twenty-six Years of the Life of an Actor and Manager.* 2 vols. New York: Burgess, Stringer, 1847.

17 WILSON, Garff B. *A History of American Acting.* Bloomington, Ind.: Indiana UP, 1966.

18 WOOD, William B. *Personal Recollections of the Stage.* Philadelphia: Baird, 1855. (Treats the Philadelphia theatre during first half of the nineteenth century.)

Studies of Technique

19 BAKER, George Pierce. *Dramatic Technique.* Boston: Houghton Mifflin, 1919. (A fundamental book on playwriting.)*

1   CHENEY, Sheldon. *The Art Theatre*. New York: Knopf, 1925. (Perceptive treatment.)

2   GASSNER, John. *Form and Idea in Modern Theatre*. New York: Dryden, 1956. (Excellent account of realism and expressionism in the theatre.)

3   GORELIK, Mordecai. *New Theatres for Old*. New York: French, 1940. (Standard work on modern stage techniques with an extensive bibliography of theatre movements.)*

4   HAMILTON, Clayton. *The Theory of the Theatre*. New York: Holt, 1939.

5   SIMONSON, Lee. *The Stage Is Set*. New York: Harcourt, Brace, 1932. (Theatrical and dramatic techniques.)

6   STEVENS, David H., ed. *Ten Talents in the American Theatre*. Norman, Okla.: U of Oklahoma P, 1957.

Special Theatrical Groups

Provincetown

7   GLASPELL, Susan. *The Road to the Temple, the Life of George Cram Cook*. New York: Stokes, 1927. (Contains interesting account of the Provincetown Theatre.)

8   GOULD, Jean. "Susan Glaspell and the Provincetown Players." *Modern American Playwrights*. New York: Dodd, Mead, 1966.

9   SIEVERS, W. David. "Suppressed Desires and the Provincetown." *Freud on Broadway*. New York: Hermitage, 1955.*

Federal Theatre

10   DAVIS, Hallie F. *Arena*. New York: Duell, Sloan & Pearce, 1940. (Account of the Federal Theatre Project.)

11   *Federal Theatre Plays*. Introduction by Hallie Flanagan. New York: Random, 1938. (Three plays financed by the Federal Theatre Project.)

12   FRENCH, Warren, ed. *The Thirties: Fiction, Poetry, Drama*. DeLand, Fla.: Edwards, 1967. (Treats Federal Theatre project.)

13   LERNER, Max. *Ideas Are Weapons*. New York: Viking, 1939. (Includes the Federal Theatre.)

14   MATHEWS, Jane De Hart. *The Federal Theatre, 1935–1939: Plays, Relief, and Politics*. Princeton, N.J.: Princeton UP, 1967.

15   RABKIN, Gerald. "The Federal Theatre: Theatre Is Men Working." *Drama and Commitment*. Bloomington, Ind.: Indiana UP, 1964.

1 WHITMAN, Willson. *Bread and Circuses: A Study of the Federal Theatre.* New York: Oxford UP, 1937.

Theatre Guild and Group Theatre

2 CLURMAN, Harold. *The Fervent Years.* New York: Knopf, 1945. (Treats the Group Theatre of the 1930's.)

3 EATON, Walter Prichard. *The Theatre Guild: The First Ten Years.* New York: Brentano, 1929. (Account of America's most important producing company.)

4 HIMELSTEIN, Morgan Y. *Drama Was a Weapon, The Left-Wing Theatre in New York, 1929–1941.* New Brunswick, N.J.: Rutgers UP, 1963. (Informative and carefully documented treatment of the Theatre Union and Group Theatre.)

5 LANGER, Lawrence. *The Magic Curtain.* New York: Dutton, 1951. (Personal recollections of the founding of the Theatre Guild.)

6 RABKIN, Gerald. "The Group Theatre: Theatre Is Collective Art." See 8.15.

Civic Theatre

7 BEEGLE, Mary Porter, and Jack R. CRAWFORD. *Community Drama and Pageantry.* New Haven: Yale UP, 1916.

8 BURLEIGH, Louise. *The Community Theatre: In Theory and Practice.* Boston: Little, Brown, 1917.

9 MAC KAYE, Percy. *The Civic Theatre in Relation to the Redemption of Leisure.* New York: Kennerley, 1912.

Others

10 BLAKE, Ben. *The Awakening of the American Theatre.* New York: Tomorrow Pub., 1935. (Treats the "left-wing" theatre of the 1930's.)

11 CAMPBELL, C. Lawthon. "Two Years Towards a National Theatre." *QJS* 36(1950): 23–26. (A review of ANTA, 1948–1950.)

12 CHENEY, Sheldon. See 8.1.

13 CHENEY, Sheldon. *The Open Air Theatre.* New York: Kennerley, 1918.

14 GARD, Robert E., Marston BALCH, and Pauline B. TEMPKIN. *Theater in America: Appraisal and Challenge.* Madison, Wis.: Dembar Ed Res Serv, 1968. (Treats community, educational, regional, and repertory theatres.)

15 GASSNER, John. "Off-Broadway, Past and Present." *Theatre at the Crossroads.* New York: Holt, Rinehart and Winston, 1960.

1 HOUGHTON, Norris. *Advance from Broadway*. New York: Harcourt, Brace, 1941. (Treats the touring road companies.)

2 NOVICK, Julius. *Beyond Broadway: The Quest for Permanent Theatres*. New York: Hill and Wang, 1968. (Valuable evaluations of theatres outside of New York.)

3 REEVES, Elizabeth W. "Defining Repertory Theatre in America." *Drama Critique* 10(1967): 25–29.

4 RICE, Elmer. "The First Decade." *TArts* 33(1949): 53–56. (Reviews the first ten years of the Playwright's Company.)

5 WEALES, Gerald. "Off-Broadway." *American Drama Since World War II*. New York: Harcourt, Brace, & World, 1962. (Excellent study.)*

Special Studies of the American Drama

By Periods

COLONIAL AND EARLY REPUBLIC

6 BROWN, Herbert R. "Sensibility in Eighteenth-Century American Drama." *AL* 4(1932): 47–60.

7 COAD, Oral S. "Stage and Players in Eighteenth Century America." *JEGP* 19(1920): 1–23.

8 COWIE, Alexander. "The Beginnings of Fiction and Drama." *Literary History of the United States*. Vol. I. Ed. by Robert E. Spiller, et al. New York: Macmillan, 1948.

9 DALY, Charles P. *First Theatre in America*. New York: Dunlap Society, 1896. (Corrects some errors in William Dunlap's important history.)

10 DUNLAP, William. *History of the American Theatre and Anecdotes of the Principal Actors*. New York: Burt Franklin, 1963. (A reprint of the 1832 edition of Dunlap's history, still valuable, as first-hand source material, to which is added "A Narrative of His Connection with the Old American Company 1792–1797" by John Hodgkinson.)*

11 FORD, Paul Leicester. *Washington and the Theatre*. New York: Dunlap Society, 1899. (Brief account of the theatre of the early republic.)

12 HEWITT, Barnard. *Theatre U.S.A.: 1668–1957*. New York: McGraw-Hill, 1959. (Contains extensive selections from contemporary critics.)

13 MOSES, Montrose J., and John Mason BROWN, eds. *The American Theatre as Seen by Its Critics*. New York: Norton, 1934. (Fine collection of dramatic criticism.)

14 QUINN, Arthur H. "The Early Drama, 1756–1860." *Cambridge History of American Literature*. Vol. I. Ed. by William P. Trent, et al. New York: Macmillan, 1933.

1 RANKIN, Hugh F. *The Theater in Colonial America*. Chapel Hill: U. of North Carolina P, 1965. (A thorough record of the repertoire and personalities of the theatrical companies from Boston to Charleston.)*

2 REES, James. *Dramatic Authors of America*. Philadelphia: Zieber, 1845. (Brief sketches.)

3 SEILHAMER, George O. *A History of the American Theatre, 1749–1797*, 3 vols. Philadelphia: Globe, 1891.

4 TYLER, Moses C. *A History of American Literature During the Colonial Period*. 2 vols. New York: Putnam, 1897. [05496, Crowell-Coll.]

5 WALDO, Lewis P. *The French Drama in America in the Eighteenth Century*. Baltimore: Johns Hopkins UP, 1942. (French influence from 1701–1800.)

NINETEENTH CENTURY

6 BRADLEY, Sculley. "The Emergence of the Modern Drama." *Literary History of the United States*. Vol. II. Ed. by Robert E. Spiller, et al. New York: Macmillan, 1948.

7 DEVLIN, James J. "William Coleman to Thomas Phillips: On the Early 19th Century American Theatres." *LCUP* 32 (1966): 40–60.

8 HAPGOOD, Norman. *The Stage in America, 1897–1900*. New York: Macmillan, 1901.

9 HEWITT, Barnard. See 10.12.

10 JOHNSON, Albert E., and W. H. CRAIN, Jr. "Dictionary of American Drama Critics, 1850–1910." *TA* 13(1955): 65–89.

11 MOSES, Montrose, J. "The Drama, 1860–1918." *Cambridge History of American Literature*. Vol. III. Ed. by William P. Trent, et al. New York: Macmillan, 1933.

12 MOSES, Montrose J., and John Mason BROWN. See 10.13.

13 QUINN, Arthur H. See 10.14.

14 REES, James. *The Dramatic Authors of America*. Philadelphia: Zieber, 1845.

15 TAUBMAN, Howard. See 6.12.

1900–1940

16 ANDREWS, Charlton. *The Drama Today*. Philadelphia: Lippincott, 1913.

17 BENTLEY, Eric. *The Playwright as Thinker*. New York: Harcourt, Brace, 1946. (Important study.)

18 BLOCK, Anita. *The Changing World in Plays and Theatre*. Boston: Little, Brown, 1939. (Dramatic and theatrical ideas of the late 1930's.)

19 BROWN, John Mason. *Two on the Aisle: Ten Years of the American Theatre in Performance*. New York: Norton, 1938.

1   BROWN, John Mason. *Upstage: The American Theatre in Performance.* New York: Norton, 1930. (Treats playwrights, actors, scenic designers, and directors of past two decades.)*

2   BURTON, Richard. *The New American Drama.* New York: Crowell, 1913.

3   CHENEY, Sheldon. *The New Movement in the Theatre.* New York: Mitchell Kennerley, 1914.

4   CLARK, Barrett H. *Intimate Portraits.* New York: Dramatists' Play Service, 1951.

5   CLARK, Barrett H. *A Study of the Modern Drama.* New York: Appleton-Century-Crofts, 1938. (A helpful handbook with an American section.)

6   CLURMAN, Harold. "The Theatre of the Thirties." TDR 4(1959): 3–11.

7   DICKINSON, Thomas H. *The Case of American Drama.* Boston: Houghton Mifflin, 1915.

8   DICKINSON, Thomas H. *Playwrights of the New American Theatre.* New York: Macmillan, 1924. (Treats the early-century dramatists.)

9   DOWNER, Alan. *Fifty Years of American Drama, 1900–1950.* Chicago: Regnery, 1951.

10   DUKES, Ashley. *The Youngest Drama.* Chicago: Sergel, 1924.

11   EATON, Walter P. *The American Stage of Today.* Boston: Small, Maynard, 1908.

12   FLEXNER, Eleanor. *American Playwrights, 1918–1938.* New York: Simon and Schuster, 1938. (Social criticism of the drama.)

13   GAGEY, Edmond. *Revolution in American Drama.* New York: Columbia UP, 1947. (Includes musicals.)

14   GASSNER, John. *Masters of the Drama.* Rev. ed. New York: Dover, 1954. (Includes American drama with European.)

15   GASSNER, John. "Playwrights of the Period." *TArts* 44 (1960): 19–22, 69, 71. (Drama of the 1930's.)

16   HALLINE, Allan G. "American Dramatic Theory Comes of Age." *Bucknell U. Stud* 1(1949): 1–11. (Theories of American drama, 1886–1949.)

17   HAMILTON, Clayton. *Problems of the Playwright.* New York: Henry Holt, 1917.

18   HEWITT, Barnard. See 10.12.

19   KRUTCH, Joseph Wood. "An American Drama." *Literary History of the United States.* Vol. II. Ed. by Robert E. Spiller, et al. New York: Macmillan, 1948.

20   KRUTCH, Joseph Wood. *The American Drama Since 1918.* Rev. ed. New York: Braziller, 1957.*

21   KRUTCH, Joseph Wood. "The Twenties: Theatre of Body and Soul." *TArts* 39(1955): 26–27, 92–94. (Spiritual considerations of the period on the stage.)

22   LEVY, H. W. "A Half Century of the Theatre." *Am. Hebrew* 160(1950): 18, 70–71, 74.

1 MANTLE, Burns. *American Playwrights of Today*. New York: Dodd, Mead, 1938. (Reviews the 1930's.)

2 MANTLE, Burns. *Contemporary American Playwrights*. New York: Dodd, Mead, 1938.

3 MERSAND, Joseph. *The American Drama Since 1930*. New York: Modern Chapbooks, 1951.

4 MOREHOUSE, Ward. "When Johnny Came Marching Home." *TArts* 43(1959): 11–14. (The American theatre in 1919.)

5 MOSES, Montrose J., and John Mason BROWN. See 10.13.

6 NATHAN, George Jean. *The Entertainment of a Nation*. New York: Knopf, 1942.

7 NATHAN, George Jean. *Passing Judgments*. New York: Knopf, 1935.

8 NATHAN, George Jean. *The Theatre Book of the Year, 1942–1943*. New York: Knopf, 1943. (Annual volumes thereafter until 1957.)

9 PHELPS, William Lyon. *Essays on American Dramatists*. New York: Macmillan, 1921.

10 RANDEL, William. "American Plays in Finland." *AL* 24(1952): 291–300. (Since 1925 Finland has continually produced American plays.)

11 SAYLER, Oliver M. *Our American Theatre, 1908–1923*. New York: Brentano, 1923.

12 STEENA, Birgitta. "The Critical Reception of American Drama in Sweden." *MD* 5(1962): 71–82. (From 1911 to 1962.)

13 STRONG, Leonard A. G. *Commonsense About the Drama*. New York: Knopf, 1937.

14 YOUNG, Stark. *Immortal Shadows*. New York: Scribner's, 1948. (A collection of sixty-five reviews, written over a twenty-five year period by an astute critic.)*

SINCE WORLD WAR II

15 BAXANDALL, Lee. "Theatre and Affliction." *Encore* 10 (1963): 8–13. (Assessment of the modern theatre, especially Albee's *Who's Afraid of Virginia Woolf?*)

16 BENTLEY, Eric. *The Dramatic Event: An American Chronicle*. New York: Horizon Press, 1954. (Appraisals by a foremost critic.)

17 BENTLEY, Eric. *In Search of Theatre*. New York: Knopf, 1953. (A foremost critic on several aspects of the theatre, including the American.)

18 BIGSBY, C. W. E. *Confrontation and Commitment: A Study of Contemporary American Drama, 1959–1966*. Columbia, Mo.: U of Missouri P, 1968. (Comprehensive, incisive criticism.)*

19 BISHOP, Thomas W. "Adaptations of American Plays in Paris, 1958–1959." *FR* 33(1960): 551–557.

20 BLOCK, Haskell, and Robert G. SHEDD. *Masters of Modern Drama*. New York: Random House, 1962. (Includes O'Neill, Odets, Saroyan, Wilder, Williams, and Miller.)

1 BLUM, Daniel, ed. *Theatre World*, 1943– . New York: Stuyvesant P, 1943– . (Series of pictorial volumes.)

2 BRUSTEIN, Robert. "Notes on a Suburban Theater." *PR* 26(1959): 593–605. (Conventions and stereotypes in the drama of the fifties.)

3 BRUSTEIN, Robert. "The Theatre Is Losing Its Mind." *Columbia U Forum* 2(1958): 15–18. (Deplores state of the drama.)

4 BRUSTEIN, Robert. *The Theatre of Revolt*. Boston: Little, Brown, 1964.

5 DOWNER, Alan. *Recent American Drama*. U of Minnesota Pamphlets No 7. Minneapolis: U of Minnesota P, 1961.

6 GAITHER, Mary, and Horst FRENZ. "German Criticism of American Drama." *AQ* 7(1955): 111–122. (Reveals enthusiastic reception of modern American plays.)

7 GARDNER, R. H. *The Splintered Stage: The Decline of the American Theater*. New York: Macmillan, 1965. (An unhappy view of the drama by the Baltimore *Sun* critic.)

8 GASSNER, John. *Directions in Modern Theatre and Drama*. New York: Holt, Rinehart, and Winston, 1965.

9 GASSNER, John. *Theatre at the Crossroads*. New York: Holt, Rinehart, and Winston, 1960. (Assesses the American dramatists at midcentury.)

10 GASSNER, John. *The Theatre in Our Time*. New York: Crown, 1954. (Particularly helpful for the forties and fifties.)*

11 GASSNER, John, and Ralph G. ALLEN. *Theatre and Drama in the Making*. Boston: Houghton Mifflin, 1964.

12 GOTTFRIED, Martin. *A Theater Divided: The Postwar American Stage*. Boston: Little, Brown, 1967. (Despite some critical flaws, offers helpful insight.)

13 GOULD, Jean. *Modern American Playwrights*. New York: Dodd, Mead, 1966. (Treats Rice, Glaspell, O'Neill, Sherwood, Anderson, Odets, Williams, Miller, Albee. Not always accurate.)

14 HALLINE, Allan G. "American Drama and World War II." *Bucknell U Stud* 2(1950): 71–79.

15 HEWES, Henry. "The American Theatre '64: Its Problems and Promises." *SR* 47(1964): 27–29, 40–42, 44–45, 50.

16 KERNODLE, George R. "Time-frightened Playwrights." *ASch* 18(1949): 446–456. (The destructive effect of the problems of the twentieth century.)

17 LAMM, Martin. *Modern Drama*. New York: Philosophical Library, 1953. (Interesting French criticism.)

18 LEWIS, Allan. *American Plays and Playwrights of the Contemporary Theatre*. New York: Crown, 1965. (Brief synoptic sketches.)

19 MC CARTHY, Mary. "Americans, Realists, Playwrights." *Encounter* 17(1961): 24–31. (On realism and American playwrights.)

20 MERSAND, Joseph. *The American Drama Since 1939*. New York: Modern Chapbooks, 1949.

1 MERSERVE, Walter, ed. *Discussions of Modern American Drama*. Boston: Heath, 1965.

2 MORGAN, Frederick. "Notes on the Theatre." *HudR* 2(1949): 269–277. (Surveys drama on Broadway in 1949.)

3 NATHAN, George Jean. "The Drama's Four Horsemen." *Am Mercury*, 45(1947): 455–460. (Blames the desolation of the drama on timeliness, journalism, cynicism, and laughs.)

4 NATHAN, George Jean. *The Magic Mirror*. New York: Knopf, 1960.

5 NATHAN, George Jean. *The Theatre in the Fifties*. New York: Knopf, 1953. (The impressions of an astute critic.)*

6 RABKIN, Gerald. See 8.15.

7 STEENA, Brigitta. See 13.12.

8 *Theatre Arts Anthology*. New York: Theatre Arts Books, 1950. (A collection of critical articles.)

9 WEALES, Gerald. "American Drama Since the Second World War." *TamR* 13(1959): 86–99.

10 WEALES, Gerald. See 10.5.

11 YOUNG, Stark. *The Flower in Drama*. New York: Scribner's, 1955. (Essays by a highly respected critic.)*

By Regions

NEW YORK

12 ATKINSON, Brooks. *Broadway Scrapbook*. New York: Theatre Arts Books, 1947. (Essays by an eminent critic for the *New York Times*.)*

13 BOYD, Alice Katharine. *The Interchange of Plays Between London and New York, 1910–1939*. New York: King's Crown Press, 1948. (Treats American plays of the period that were popular in London.)

14 BROWN, John Mason. *As They Appear*. New York: McGraw-Hill, 1952. (Perceptive essays, mostly about the theatre of 1950–1952.)

15 BROWN, John Mason. *Broadway in Review*. New York: Norton, 1940. (The New York theatre of the 1930's.)

16 BROWN, John Mason. *Dramatis Personae*. New York: Viking, 1963. [C171-Viking.] (The New York stage from 1920 in retrospect.)*

17 BROWN, John Mason. *Seeing More Things*. New York: McGraw-Hill, 1948. (Reviews the New York theatrical season of 1947–1948.)

18 BROWN, John Mason. *Seeing Things*. New York: McGraw-Hill, 1946. (Covers the New York stage, 1942–1946.)

19 BROWN, John Mason. *Still Seeing Things*. New York: McGraw-Hill, 1950. (The New York stage from 1948 to 1950.)

20 BROWN, T. Allston. *A History of the New York Stage*. 3 vols. New York: Dodd, Mead, 1903.

21 BRUSTEIN, Robert. "The Theater of Middle Seriousness: A Report on the Broadway Season." *Harper's* 218(1959): 56–63.

22 CAMPBELL, Oscar J. "The Pulitzer Prizes, 1917–1957: Drama Awards." *CLC* 6(1957): 34–36.

1 CORDELL, R. A., and Lowell MATSON, eds. *The Off-Broadway Theatre.* New York: Random, 1959. (A collection of plays given by off-Broadway groups.)

2 DOWNER, Alan S. "The New Group: Notes on the New York Theatre 1964–1965." *QJS* 51(1965): 245–257.

3 GASSNER, John. "Aspects of the Broadway Theatre." *QJS* 35(1949): 289–296. (Realism in the theatre.)

4 GASSNER, John. See 9.15.

5 IRELAND, Joseph N. *Records of the New York Stage.* 2 vols. New York: Morrell, 1866. (The first comprehensive account.)

6 NATHAN, George Jean. *Art of the Night.* New York: Knopf, 1928. (Varied personal reactions.)

7 NATHAN, George Jean. *The Morning After the First Night.* New York: Knopf, 1938.

8 *New York Theatre Critics' Reviews.* New York: Critics' Theatre Reviews 1940– . (A weekly series of reviews of the New York stage.)*

9 ODELL, George C. D. See 6.11.

10 ODELL, George C. D. "Some Theatrical Stock Companies of New York." *TA* 9(1951): 7–26.

11 PRICE, Julia S. *The Off-Broadway Theater.* New York: Scarecrow Press, 1962. (Comprehensive treatment from 1905 to 1960.)

12 SHANK, Theodore J. "Theatre for the Majority: Its Influence on a Nineteenth-Century American Theatre." *ETJ* 11(1959): 188–199. (The Bowery Theatre, 1826–1836.)

13 TOOHEY, John L. *A History of the Pulitzer Prize Plays.* New York: Citadel, 1967.

BOSTON AND NEW ENGLAND

14 ALDEN, J. "A Season in Federal Street: J. B. Williamson and the Boston Theatre, 1796–1797." *PAAS* 65(1955): 12–74. (Archives of the Federal Street Theatre.)

15 BLAKE, Charles. *An Historical Account of the Providence Stage.* Providence, R.I.: Whitney, 1868.

16 CLAPP, William W., Jr. *A Record of the Boston Stage.* Boston: James Munroe, 1853. (New England theatre before 1850.)

17 DEUTSCH, Helen, and Stella HANAU. *The Provincetown: A Story of the Theatre.* New York: Farrar, Straus, and Cudahy, 1931. (A complete account of the Provincetown Players.)

18 GLASPELL, Susan. See 8.7.

19 MARSHALL, Eleanor W. "The Weston Playhouse: Regional Drama Center." *VtQ* 15(1947): 121–124. (Cites performances of early native dramas.)

20 QUINN, Arthur H. See 6.3.

21 RYAN, Pat M. "The Old Salem Theatre." *Essex Inst Hist Coll* 98(1962): 287–293. (The theatre in Salem, Mass.)

1 SHERMAN, Constance D. "The Theatre in Rhode Island Before the Revolution." *RIH* 17(1958): 10–14.

2 TOMPKINS, Eugene, and Quincy KILBY. *The History of the Boston Theatre, 1854–1901.* Boston: Houghton Mifflin, 1908.

3 WILLARD, George O. *History of the Providence Stage, 1762–1891.* Providence, R.I.: R.D. News, 1891.

4 WOODRUFF, John. "America's Oldest Living Theatre—the Howard Athenaeum." *TA* 7(1950): 71–81. (The Howard Theatre in Boston since 1846.)

PHILADELPHIA

5 POLLOCK, Thomas Clark. *The Philadelphia Theatre in the Eighteenth Century.* Philadelphia: U of Pennsylvania P, 1933.

6 REED, James D. *Old Drury of Philadelphia.* Philadelphia: U of Pennsylvania P, 1932. (Covers the period 1800–1835.)

7 WILSON, Arthur Herman. *A History of the Philadelphia Theatre, 1835–1855.* Philadelphia: U of Pennsylvania P, 1935.

8 WOOD, William B. See 7.18.

THE SOUTH

9 ADAMS, Henry W. *The Montgomery Theatre, 1822–1835.* University, Ala.: U of Alabama P, 1955.

10 ARMISTEAD, Margaret B. "The Savannah Theater—Oldest in America." *GaR* 7(1953): 50–56. (History of a theatre, built in 1818.)

11 BROCKETT, O. G. "The Theatre of the Southern United States from the Beginnings through 1865: A Bibliographical Essay." *Theatre Research* 2(1960): 163–174.

12 DORMAN, James H., Jr. *Theater in the Ante Bellum South, 1815–1861.* Chapel Hill, N.C.: U of North Carolina P, 1967. (Good historical survey.)*

13 FIFE, Oline. "The Confederate Theater in Georgia." *GaR* 9(1955): 305–315.

14 GALLEGLY, Joseph S. "The Renaissance of the Galveston Theatre: Henry Greenwall's First Season, 1867–1868." *SHQ*, 62(1959): 442–456.

15 GOWER, Herschel. "Nashville's Community Playhouse." *Holland's Mag* 67(1948): 10–11.

16 GRAHAM, Philip. *Showboat.* Austin, Tex.: U of Texas P, 1951. (History of the river showboats and their plays.)

17 HARWELL, R. B. "Civil War Theater: The Richmond Stage." *Civil War Hist.* 1(1955): 295–304.

18 HERRON, Ima H. "Home Grown Plays." *SWR* 34(1949): 202–215. (Regional drama in the South.)

19 HOOLE, W. Stanley. *The Ante-bellum Charleston Theatre.* Tuscaloosa, Ala.: U of Alabama P, 1946.

20 JONES, Margo. *Theatre in the Round.* New York: Rinehart, 1951. (Arena staging in Dallas, Texas.)

1   KENDALL, John S. *The Golden Age of the New Orleans Theater*. Baton Rouge: Louisiana State UP, 1952. (From about 1845 to around 1880.)*

2   LAND, Robert H. "The First Williamsburg Theater." *WMQ*, 3rd ser. 5(1948): 359–374.

3   LE GARDEUR, René J., Jr. *The First New Orleans Theatre 1792–1803*. New Orleans: Leeward, 1963.

4   PARKER, John W. *Adventures in Playmaking*. Chapel Hill, N.C.: U of North Carolina P, 1959. (Original plays produced by the Carolina Playmakers.)

5   ROSENFIELD, John. "The Resident Arts: Villain Still Pursues Her." *SWR* 34(1949): 320–335; 395–398. (Theatrical groups in Dallas from the twenties through the forties.)

6   RULFS, Donald J. "The Ante-Bellum Professional Theater in Raleigh." *NCHR* 29(1952): 344–358.

7   RULFS, Donald J. "The Professional Theater in Wilmington, 1858–1870." *NCHR* 28(1951): 119–136.

8   RULFS, Donald J. "The Professional Theater in Wilmington, 1870–1900." *NCHR* 28(1951): 315–331.

9   RULFS, Donald J. "The Professional Theater in Wilmington, 1900–1934." *NCHR* 28(1951): 463–486. (Thirty-five years of a North Carolina theatre.)

10 RULFS, Donald J. "The Theater in Asheville from 1879 to 1931." *NCHR* 36(1959): 429–441.

11 SHOCKLEY, Martin S. "The Richmond Theatre, 1780–1790'" *VMHB* 60(1952): 421–436.*

12 WALSER, Richard, ed. *North Carolina Drama*. Richmond: Garrett & Massie, 1956. (Includes plays by Paul Green and Thomas Wolfe. The introduction is a history of drama in North Carolina.)

13 WILLIS, Eola. *The Charleston Stage of the 18th Century*. Columbia, S.C.: State, 1924.

MIDDLE WEST

14 BRIGGS, Harold E., and Ernestine B. "The Early Theatre on the Northern Plains." *Mississippi Valley Hist Rev* 37(1950): 231–264. (Pioneer theatrical activities in Iowa, Montana, the Dakotas, and Wyoming.)

15 CARSON, William G. B. *Managers in Distress: The St. Louis Stage, 1840–1844*. St. Louis: St. Louis Historical Documents Foundation, 1949.

16 CARSON, William G. B. *The Theatre on the Frontier*. Chicago: U of Chicago P, 1932. (Early performances in St. Louis.)

17 DRAEGERT, Eva. "The Theater in Indianapolis before 1880." *Ind Mag of Hist*, 51(1955): 121–138.

18 FLORY, Julia McCune. *The Cleveland Play House: How It Began*. Cleveland, Ohio: Western Reserve UP, 1965. (Covers the years 1915–1927.)

19 GUTHRIE, Tyrone. *A New Theatre*. New York: McGraw-Hill, 1964. (The establishment of a professional repertory company in Minneapolis.)

1   MALIN, James C. "Early Theatre at Fort Scott." *KHQ* 24(1958): 31–56.

2   MALIN, James C. "Theatre in Kansas, 1858–1868." *KHQ* 23(1957): 191–203.

3   MC DAVITT, Elaine E. "The Beginnings of Theatrical Activities in Detroit." *MichH* 31(1947): 35–47.

4   MILLER, James Albert. *The Detroit Yiddish Theater, 1920–1937.* Detroit: Wayne State UP, 1967.

5   SCHICK, Joseph S. "The Early Theater in Davenport, Iowa." *Palimpsest* 31(1950): 1–44.

6   SCHICK, Joseph S. *The Early Theater in Eastern Iowa.* Chicago: U of Chicago P, 1939. (Rise of the theatre in Davenport and eastern Iowa, 1836–1863.)

FAR WEST

7   DAVIS, Ronald L. "They Played for Gold: Theater on the Mining Frontier." *SWR* 51(1966): 169–184.

8   DE la TORRE, Lillian. "The Theatre Comes to Denver." *ColM* 37(1960): 285–296.

9   GAGEY, Edmund M. *The San Francisco Stage.* New York: Columbia UP, 1950. (Contains valuable facts.)*

10 HENDERSON, Myrtle E. *History of the Theatre in Salt Lake City.* Salt Lake City, Utah: Deseret, 1941.

11 MAC MINN, George R. *The Theatre of the Golden Era of California.* Caldwell, Idaho: Caxton, 1941.

12 PYPER, George D. *The Romance of an Old Playhouse.* Salt Lake City, Utah: Seagull P, 1928. (The Salt Lake City Theatre.)

13 RAY, Terry. "The Albuquerque Little Theatre: Its 30 Years." *NMQ* 30(1960): 11–25.

14 SCHOBERLIN, Melvin. *From Candles to Footlights: A Biography of the Pike's Peak Theatre, 1859–1876.* Denver, Colorado: Rosenstock, 1941.

By Genre

VERSE DRAMA

15 ANDERSON, Maxwell. "A Prelude to Poetry in the Theatre." *Winterset.* Washington, D.C.: Anderson, 1935.

16 DONOGHUE, Denis. *The Third Voice: Modern British and American Verse Drama.* Princeton, N.J.: Princeton UP, 1959. [64-Princeton.]*

17 ELIOT, T. S. *Poetry and Drama.* Cambridge, Mass.: Harvard UP, 1953. (Affirms modern poetic drama.)*

18 GERSTENBERGER, Donna. "Verse Drama in America: 1916–1939." See 15.1.

19 PEACOCK, Ronald. *The Poet in the Theatre.* New York: Hill and Wang, 1960.

TRAGEDY

1   ANDERSON, Maxwell. *The Essence of Tragedy*. Washington, D.C.: Anderson, 1939. (A penetrating essay by an important playwright.)*

2   BROUSSARD, Louis. *American Drama: Contemporary Allegory from Eugene O'Neill to Tennessee Williams*. Norman: U of Oklahoma P, 1962. (Treats man's struggle in a world dominated by materialism and bureaucracy.)

3   BROWN, John Mason. "The Tragic Blueprint." See 15.16.*

4   GASSNER, John. "Tragedy in the Modern Theatre." See 14.10.

5   MC COLLOM, W. G. *Tragedy*. New York: Macmillan, 1957. (Not strictly American, but helpful.)

6   MILSTEAD, John. "The Structure of Modern Tragedy." *WHR* 12(1958): 365–369.

7   O'HARA, Frank H. *Today in American Drama*. Chicago: U of Chicago P, 1939. (Treats the drama briefly by types.)

8   SKINNER, R. Dana. *Our Changing Theatre*. New York: Dial, 1931. (Brief appraisals by types.)

COMEDY

9   COLBY, Elbridge. *Early American Comedy*. New York: New York Public Library, 1919.

10   HARTMAN, John Geoffrey. *The Development of American Social Comedy, 1787–1936*. Philadelphia: U of Pennsylvania P, 1939.

11   QUINN, Arthur H. See 6.3.

FOLK DRAMA

12   KOCH, Frederick H., ed. *American Folk Plays*. New York: Appleton-Century, 1939. (Illustrates the making of folk plays.)*

13   KOCH, Frederick H., ed. *Carolina Folk-Plays*. New York: Henry Holt, 1941.

14   SPER, Felix. *From Native Roots: A Panorama of Our Regional Drama* Caldwell, Idaho: Caxton, 1948.

15   WALSER, Richard. *North Carolina Drama*. Richmond, Va.: Garrett and Massie, 1956. (Ten regional plays.)

POPULAR FORM

16   BIRDOFF, Harry. *The World's Greatest Hit: Uncle Tom's Cabin*. New York: Vanni, 1947.

17   DISHER, M. Willson. *Melodrama: Plots That Thrilled*. London: Rockliff, 1954. (Good discussion of the type; includes several American plays.)

18   GRIMSTEAD, David. *Melodrama Unveiled: American Theater and Culture, 1800–1850*. Chicago: U of Chicago P, 1968. (Reveals the cultural climate that made melodrama popular.)

19   HEWITT, Barnard. "Uncle Tom and Uncle Sam: New Light on an Old Play." *QJS* 27(1951): 63–70. (George L. Aiken's dramatization of Mrs. Stowe's *Uncle Tom's Cabin*.)

1 ISAACS, E. J. R., and Rosamond GILDER. "Theatre with Father." *TArts* 27(1943): 459–503.

2 RAHILL, Frank. "America's Number One Hit." *TArts*, 36(Oct., 1952), 18–24. (Theatrical history of *Uncle Tom's Cabin*.)

3 RAHILL, Frank. *The World of Melodrama*. University Park, Pa.: Penn State UP, 1968.

4 VARDAC, A. Nicholas. *Stage to Screen: Theatrical Method from Garrick to Griffith*. Cambridge: Harvard UP, 1949. (Discusses melodrama and spectacle plays.)

By Theme or Subject

5 BERGMAN, Herbert. "Major Civil War Plays, 1882–1899." *Southern Speech Jour* 19(1954): 224–231.

6 BEYER, William H. "The State of the Theatre: The Strindberg Heritage." *School and Society* 71(1950): 23–28.

7 BOND, Frederick W. *The Negro and the Drama*. Washington, D.C.: Associated, 1940.

8 BOOTH, Michael R. "The Drunkard's Progress: Nineteenth Century Temperance Drama." *DR* 44(1964): 205–212. (Treats a popular theme of the period.)

9 BROUSSARD, Louis. See 20.2.

10 COUCH, William, Jr. *New Black Playwrights: An Anthology*. Baton Rouge: Louisiana State UP, 1969. (Six plays by avant-garde playwrights.)

11 DUSENBURY, Winifred L. *The Theme of Loneliness in Modern American Drama*. Gainesville: U of Florida P, 1960.

12 FINKELSTEIN, Sidney. *Existentialism and Alienation in American Literature*. New York: International, 1965.

13 GASSNER, John. *Form and Idea in Modern Theatre*. New York: Dryden, 1956. (Discusses realism and expressionism.)*

14 GASSNER, John. "Reasons for Social Drama." See 14.9.

15 GOLDBERG, Isaac. *The Drama of Transition*. Cincinnati, Ohio: Stewart Kidd, 1922. (Treats the new American realism.)

16 HERRON, Ima H. *The Small Town in American Drama*. Dallas, Tex.: Southern Methodist UP, 1969. (Treats over 300 plays, showing different regions, themes, techniques.)

17 HODGE, Francis. *Yankee Theatre: The Image of America on the Stage, 1825–1850*. Austin: U of Texas P, 1964.

18 HUTTON, Laurence. *Curiosities of the American Stage*. New York: Hooper, 1891. (Treats native themes.)

19 ISAACS, Edith J. R. *The Negro in the American Theatre*. New York: Theatre Arts, 1947.

20 KOSTER, Donald N. *The Theme of Divorce in American Drama, 1871–1939*. Philadelphia: U of Penn, 1942.

21 KRUTCH, Joseph Wood. *Modernism in Modern Drama*. Ithaca, N.Y.: Cornell UP, 1953. (Comments on subject matter.)

1 LOCKE, Alain, ed. *Plays of Negro Life*. New York: Harper, 1927. (Collection of twenty plays about Negroes.)

2 LYNCH, William F. "Ritual and Drama." *Cweal* 71(1960): 586–588.

3 MAC KAYE, Percy. *The Playhouse and the Play*. New York: Macmillan, 1909. (Concerns the theatre and democracy.)

4 MERSAND, Joseph. "The Drama of Social Significance." See 14.20.

5 MERSAND, Joseph. "Two Decades of Biographical Plays." See 14.20.

6 MITCHELL, Loften. *Black Drama*. New York: Hawthorn, 1967. (Surveys the Negro on the American stage.)

7 MOODY, Richard. *America Takes the Stage: Romanticism in American Drama and Theatre, 1750–1900*. Bloomington: Indiana UP, 1955. (Good for native themes.)

8 NANNES, Caspar. *Politics in the American Drama*. Washington, D.C.: Catholic U of America P, 1960. (Treats the drama as a mirror of increased sophistication in politics.)

9 O'HARA, Frank H. *Today in American Drama*. Chicago: U of Chicago P, 1939. (Treats contemporary themes.)

10 RABKIN, Gerald. "Politics in the American Theatre of the Thirties." See 8.15.

11 ROPPOLO, Joseph P. "American Themes, Heroes, and History on the New Orleans Stage, 1806–1865." *TSE* 5(1955): 151–181.

12 SHIRK, Samuel B. *The Characterization of George Washington in American Plays*. Easton, Pa.: Correll, 1949. (Contains summaries of plots and a list of plays.)

13 SIEVERS, W. David. See 8.9.

14 SPER, Felix. "Early Types." See 20.14.

15 SPER, Felix. "The Negro Theme." See 20.14.

16 WALBRIDGE, Earle F. "Drames á Clef: A List of Plays with Characters Based on Real People. Part II: American Drama." *BNYPL* 60(1956): 235–247.

17 WALSER, Richard. "Negro Dialect in Eighteenth-Century American Drama." *AS* 30(1955): 269–276.

18 WITTKE, Carl. "The Immigrant Theme on the American Stage." *Miss Val Hist Rev* 39(1952): 211–232.

Major American Dramatists

Albee, Edward (1928–   )

19 *Three Plays* by Edward Albee. New York: Coward-McCann, 1960. (Introduction by the author.)

20 ALBEE, Edward. "Which Theatre Is the Absurd One?" See 15.1.

21 CAPPELLETTI, John. "Are You Afraid of Edward Albee?" *Drama Critique*, 6(1963), 84–88.

1 CHESTER, Alfred. "Edward Albee: Red Herrings and White Whales." *Commentary* 35(1963): 296–301.

2 DANIEL, Walter C. "Absurdity in *The Death of Bessie Smith*." *CLAJ* 8(1964): 78–80.

3 DEBUSCHER, Gilbert. *Edward Albee: Tradition and Renewal*. Brussels, Belgium: American Studies Center, 1967. (Excellent analyses of themes, symbols, and structure.)

4 FRUCHTER, Norm. "Albee's Broadway Break-Thru." *Encore* 10(1963): 44–48.

5 GALEY, Matthieu. "Albee sur le chemin de la gloire." *NL* 43(1965): 13.

6 GOULD, Jean. "Edward Albee and the Current Scene." See 14.13.

7 HAMILTON, Kenneth. "Mr. Albee's Dream." *QQ* 70(1963): 393–399.

8 HARRIS, Wendell V. "Morality, Absurdity, and Albee." *SWR* 49(1964): 249–256.

9 KOSTELANETZ, Richard. "Albee's 'Sad Cafe'." *SR* 72(1964): 724–726.

10 LEWIS, Allan. "The Fun and Games of Edward Albee." See 14.18.

11 LEWIS, Allan. "The Fun and Games of Edward Albee." *ETJ* 16(1964): 29–39.

12 LYONS, Charles R. "Two Projections of the Isolation of the Human Soul: Brecht and Albee." *DramS* 4(1965): 121–138.*

13 MC DONALD, Daniel. "Truth and Illusion in *Who's Afraid of Virginia Woolf?*" *Renascence* 17(1964): 63–69.

14 MEYER, Ruth. "Language: Truth and Illusion in *Who's Afraid of Virginia Woolf?*" *ETJ* 20(1968): 60–69.

15 OBERG, A. K. "Edward Albee: His Language and Imagination." *PrS*, 40(1966): 139–146.

16 PLOTINSKY, Melvin L. "The Transformations of Understanding: Edward Albee in the Theatre of the Irresolute." *DramS* 4(1965): 220–232.

17 ROY, Emil. "*Who's Afraid of Virginia Woolf?* and the Tradition." *BuR* 13(1965): 27–36.

18 SAPONTA, Marc. "Edward Albee." *Informations et Documents* 187(1963): 20–22. (An interview.)

19 WELLWARTH, George. *The Theatre of Protest and Paradox*. New York: New York UP, 1964. [NYU-Pr.] (The final chapter deals with Albee.)

20 WHITBREAD, Thomas B., ed. *Seven Contemporary Authors*. Austin: U of Texas P, 1967. (Includes Albee.)

21 WITHERINGTON, Paul. "Language of Movement in Albee's 'The Death of Bessie Smith'." *TCL* 13(1967): 84–88.

22 ZIMBARDO, Rose A. "Symbolism and Naturalism in Edward Albee's *The Zoo Story*." *TCL* 8(1962): 10–17.

Anderson, Maxwell (1888–1959)

1 *Eleven Verse Plays* by Maxwell Anderson. New York: Harcourt, Brace, 1940.

2 ABERNETHY, Francis E. " 'Winterset': A Modern Revenge Tragedy." *MD* 7(1964): 185–189.

3 ANDERSON, Maxwell. *The Essence of Tragedy and Other Footnotes and Papers.* New York: Anderson, 1939.

4 ANDERSON, Maxwell. *Off Broadway: Essays About the Theatre.* New York: Barnes & Noble, 1947. (Dramatic theories of a leading playwright.)*

5 AVERY, Laurence G. "Maxwell Anderson: A Changing Attitude toward Love." *MD* 10(1967): 241–248.

6 BAILEY, Mabel Driscoll. *Maxwell Anderson: The Playwright as Prophet.* New York: Abelard-Schuman, 1957.

7 CARMER, Carl. "Maxwell Anderson: Poet and Champion." *TArts Monthly* 17(1933): 437–446. (Traces Anderson's development as a dramatist and a crusading spirit.)

8 CHILDS, H. E. "Playgoer's Playwright: Maxwell Anderson." *EJ* 27(1938): 475–485.

9 CLARK, Barrett H. *Maxwell Anderson: The Man and His Plays.* New York: French, 1933.*

10 COLLIUN, Gustaf. "Maxwell Anderson." *Bonniers Litterära Magasin* (Stockholm) 9(1940): 689–693.

11 COX, Martha. *Maxwell Anderson Bibliography.* Charlottesville: Bibliographical Society of Virginia, 1958. (Includes reviews of the plays.)*

12 DUSENBURY, Winifred L. "Winterset." See 21.11.

13 GAGEY, Edmond M. See 12.13.

14 GASSNER, John. "Maxwell Anderson: The Poet in Show Business." See 14.10.*

15 GILBERT, Vedder M. "The Career of Maxwell Anderson: A Check List of Books and Articles." *MD* 2(1960): 386–394.

16 GOULD, Jean. "Maxwell Anderson." See 14.13.

17 HALLINE, A. G. "Maxwell Anderson's Dramatic Theory." *AL* 16(1944): 63–81.

18 HARRIS, Ainslie. "Maxwell Anderson." *Madison Quar* 4(1944): 30–44. (Analysis of the tragedies.)

19 HEALEY, R. C. "Anderson, Saroyan, Sherwood: New Directions." *CathW* 152(1940): 174–180.

20 KLIGER, Samuel. "Hebraic Lore in Maxwell Anderson's *Winterset*." *AL* 18(1946): 219–232.

21 KRUTCH, Joseph W. "The Poetic Drama: Maxwell Anderson." See 12.20.*

22 LEE, Henry G. "Maxwell Anderson's Impact on the Theatre." *NDQ* 25(1957): 49–52.

23 MAGUIRE, C. E. "The Divine Background." *Drama Critique* 2(1959): 18–33. (Discusses *Mary of Scotland*.)

1 MILESTEAD, John. "Structure of Modern Tragedy." See 20.6.

2 NATHAN, George Jean. "After-Thoughts on Playwrights." See 16.7.

3 NATHAN, George Jean. "Maxwell Anderson." See 15.5.

4 *NDQ* 25(1957). (Special Maxwell Anderson issue.)

5 PEARCE, Howard D. "Job in Anderson's *Winterset*." *MD* 6(1963), 32–41. (Attempts to parallel the play with the book of Job.)

6 PRIOR, Moody E. *The Language of Tragedy*. New York: Columbia UP, 1947. (Treatment of Anderson's verse.)

7 RABKIN, Gerald. "The Political Paradox of Maxwell Anderson." See 8.15.

8 RICE, Patrick J. "Maxwell Anderson and the Eternal Dream." *CathW* 177(1953): 364–370.

9 RIEPE, Dale. "The Philosophy of Maxwell Anderson." *NDQ* 24(1956): 45–50.

10 ROBERTSON, C. L. "In the Days of Peg Top Trousers." *NDQ* 25(1957): 52–54. (Recollections of Anderson in college.)

11 ROBY, Robert C. "Two Worlds: Maxwell Anderson's *Winterset*." *CE* 18(1957): 195–202.

12 RODELL, J. S. "Maxwell Anderson: A Criticism." *KR* 5(1943): 272–277.

13 ROSENBERG, Harold. "Poetry and the Theatre." *Poetry* 57(1941): 258–263.

14 SAMPLEY, Arthur M. "Theory and Practice in Maxwell Anderson's Poetic Tragedies." *CE* 5(1944): 412–418.*

15 SEDGWICK, Ruth W. "Maxwell Anderson." *The Stage* 14(1936): 54–56. (Stresses the importance of dramatic poetry.)

16 SHERWOOD, Robert E. " 'White Desert' to 'Bad Seed'." *TArts* 39(March, 1955): 28–29, 93. (Acclaim for Anderson's career.)*

17 SIEVERS, W. David. "Maxwell Anderson." See 8.9.

18 STEINER, Pauline, and Horst FRENZ. "Anderson and Stallings' *What Price Glory?* and Carl Zuckmayer's *Rivalen*." *GQ* 20(1947): 239–251. (Compares the German translation with the original.)

19 WALL, Vincent. "Maxwell Anderson: The Last Anarchist." *SR* 49(1941): 339–369.

20 WATTS, H. H. "Maxwell Anderson: The Tragedy of Attrition." *CE* 4(1943): 220–230.

21 WOODBRIDGE, H. E. "Maxwell Anderson." *SAQ* 44(1945): 55–68.

Barry, Philip (1896–1949)

22 BROUSSARD, Louis. "Philip Barry." See 20.2.

23 BROWN, John Mason. "The American Barry." See 15.19.

24 BROWN, John Mason. "America Speaks." See 11.19.

25 BROWN, John Mason. "The Playwright and the American Theatre." See 12.1.

1   CARMER, Carl. "Philip Barry." *TArts Monthly* 13(1929): 819–826.

2   CLARK, Barrett H. "Philip Barry: The Development of a Distinguished Dramatic Talent." *Theatre Guild Magazine* 7(1930): 21.

3   DICKINSON, Donald H. "Mr. Eliot's *Hotel Universe*." *Drama Critique* 1(1958): 33–44. (Compares *The Cocktail Party* with Barry's *Hotel Universe*.)

4   DUSENBURY, Winifred L. "The Failure of a Love Affair." See 21.11.

5   FLEXNER, Eleanor. "Philip Barry." See 12.12.

6   GASSNER, John. "Philip Barry: A Civilized Playwright." See 14.10.*

7   GOULD, Jean. "Philip Barry." See 14.13.

8   HAMM, Gerald. *The Drama of Philip Barry*. Philadelphia: Privately Printed, 1948.

9   KRUTCH, Joseph W. "Comedy." See 12.20.

10   LAVERY, Emmet. "The World of Philip Barry." *Drama Critique* 3(1960): 98–107.

11   LIPPMAN, Monroe. "Philip Barry and His Socio-Political Attitudes." *QJS* 42(1956): 151–156.

12   MANTLE, Burns. "Philip Barry." See 13.1.

13   QUINN, Arthur H. "The New Decade." See 6.3.

14   ROPPOLO, Joseph P. *Philip Barry*. New York: Twayne, 1965. (Biographical and critical.)

15   SIEVERS, W. David. "The Psychodramas of Philip Barry." See 8.9.*

Behrman, S[amuel] N[athaniel] (1893–   )

16   *Three Plays* by S. N. Behrman. New York: Farrar & Rinehart, 1934.

17   *Four Plays* by S. N. Behrman. New York: Random, 1955.

18   BROWN, John Mason. "S. N. Behrman as a Comic Dramatist." See 11.19.*

19   FLEXNER, Eleanor. "S. N. Behrman." See 12.12.

20   GASSNER, John. "S. N. Behrman: Comedy and Tolerance." See 14.10.

21   KAPLAN, Charles. "S. N. Behrman: The Quandry of the Comic Spirit." *CE* 11(1950): 317–323.

22   KRUTCH, Joseph W. "Comedy." See 12.20.

23   LEWIS, Allan. "The Tired Deans—Elmer Rice and S. N. Behrman." See 14.18.

24   MANTLE, Burns. "S. N. Behrman." See 13.2.

25   MERSAND, Joseph. "S. N. Behrman and the American Comedy of Manners." *Players' Mag* 17(1941): 6–8.

26   NATHAN, George Jean. "S. N. Behrman." See 15.5.

27   QUINN, Arthur H. "The New Decade, 1927–1936." See 6.3.

28   RABKIN, Gerald. "S. N. Behrman: No Time for Comedy?" See 8.15.

1 SIEVERS, W. David. "Drawing Room Freudians—Behrman." See 8.9.

2 WEALES, Gerald. "S. N. Behrman Comes Home. 'The Worcester Account' on Broadway." *Commentary* 27(1959): 256–260.

Boker, George Henry (1823–1890)

3 *Plays and Poems* by George Henry Boker. 2 vols. Philadelphia: Lippincott, 1883.

4 *Glaucus & Other Plays* by George Henry Boker. Ed. by Sculley Bradley. Princeton, N.J.: Princeton UP, 1940.

5 BEATTY, Richmond C. "Bayard Taylor and George H. Boker." *AL* 6(1934): 316–327.

6 BRADLEY, Edward Sculley. *George Henry Boker: Poet and Patriot.* Philadelphia: U of Pennsylvania P, 1927. (Authoritative, fully documented.)*

7 BRADLEY, Sculley. "George Henry Boker and Angie Hicks." *AL* 8(1936): 258–265.

8 BRADLEY, Sculley. "Poe on the New York Stage in 1855." *AL* 9(1937): 353–354. (Shows influence of Poe on Boker's *The Bankrupt*.)

9 *Chronicle of the Union League of Philadelphia*. Philadelphia: Privately Published, 1902.

10 CONRAD, R. T. "Boker's Leonor de Guzman." *Graham's Magazine* 44(1854): 273.

11 HUBBELL, Jay B. "George Henry Boker, Paul Hamilton Hayne, and Charles Warren Stoddard: Some Unpublished Letters." *AL* 5(1933): 146–165.

12 KRUTCH, Joseph Wood. "George Henry Boker, a Little Known American Dramatist." *SR* 25(1917): 457–468.*

13 METCALF, John Calvin. "An Old Romantic Triangle: Francesca da Rimini in Three Dramas." *SR* 29(1921): 45–58.

14 MOSES, Montrose J. "George H. Boker." See 6.1.

15 QUINN, Arthur H. "The Dramas of George Henry Boker." *PMLA* 32(1917): 233–266.*

16 QUINN, Arthur H. "George Henry Boker and the Later Romantic Tragedy." See 6.2.

17 QUINN, Arthur H. "George Henry Boker—Playwright and Patriot." *Scribner's* 73(1923): 701–715.

18 *Reception Tendered by the Union League of Philadelphia to George H. Boker*. Philadelphia: Collins, 1872.

19 TAYLOR, G. H. "Check List to Writings by and about George H. Boker (1823–1890)." *ABC* 5(1934): 372–374.

20 *Twenty-fifth Anniversary of the Organization of the Union League of Philadelphia*. Lippincott: Philadelphia, 1888.

21 URBAN, Gertrude. "Paolo and Francesca in History and Literature." *Critic* 40(1902): 425–438.

Connelly, Marc[us] Cook (1890–   )

1   CONNELLY, Marc. *Voices Offstage*. New York: Holt, Rinehart and Winston, 1968.

2   DICKINSON, Thomas H. "Modern Domestic Comedy: Kaufman and Connelly." See 12.8.

3   FLEXNER, Eleanor. "Marc Connelly." See 12.12.

4   FORD, Nick A. "How Genuine is *The Green Pastures?*" *Phylon* 20(1959): 67–70.

5   GAGEY, Edmond M. See 12.13.

6   KRUMPELMANN, John T. "Marc Connelly's *The Green Pastures* and Goethe's *Faust*." *LSUSHS* 2(1962): 199–218.

7   MANTLE, Burns. See 13.1.

8   MANTLE, Burns. See 13.2.

9   NOLAN, Paul T. "God on Stage: A Problem in Characterization, Marc Connelly's Green Pastures." *XUS* 4(1965): 75–84.

10   QUINN, Arthur H. "The New Realism of Character." See 6.3.

11   WITHINGTON, Robert. "Notes on the Corpus Christi Plays and 'The Green Pastures'." *Shakespeare Assn Bul* 9(1934): 193–197.

12   YOUNG, Stark. "The Green Pastures." *New Republic* 42(1930): 128–129.

13   YOUNG, Stark. See 13.14.

Crothers, Rachel (1878–1958)

14   CROTHERS, Rachel. "The Construction of a Play." *The Art of Playwrighting*. Philadelphia: U of Pennsylvania P, 1928.

15   DICKINSON, Thomas H. "Rachel Crothers." See 12.8.

16   EATON, Walter P. *At the New Theatre and Others*. Boston: Small, Maynard, 1910. (Treats Miss Crother's early plays.)

17   FLEXNER, Eleanor. "Rachel Crothers." See 12.12.

18   GAGEY, Edmond M. See 12.13.

19   MANTLE, Burns. "Rachel Crothers." See 13.2.

20   QUINN, Arthur H. "Rachel Crothers and the Feminine Criticism of Life." See 6.3.

Eliot, T[homas] S[tearns] (1888–1965)

21   ELIOT, T. S. *The Complete Poems and Plays*. New York: Harcourt, Brace, 1952.

22   ADAIR, Patricia M. "Mr. Eliot's *Murder in the Cathedral*." *Cambridge Jour* 4(1950): 83–95.

1   ARROWSMITH, William. "English Verse Drama II: The Cocktail Party." *HudR* 3(1950): 411–431.

2   BALAKANIAN, Nona. "Affirmation and Love in Eliot." *New Leader* 42(1959): 20–21. (On *The Elder Statesman*.)

3   BARTH, J. Robert. "T. S. Eliot's Image of Man: A Thematic Study of His Drama." *Renascence* 14(1962): 126–138, 165.

4   BATTENHOUSE, Roy W. "Eliot's 'The Family Reunion' as Christian Prophecy." *Christendom* 10(1945): 307–321.

5   BRAYBROOKE, Neville, ed. *T. S. Eliot: A Symposium for His Seventieth Birthday*. London: Hart-Davis, 1958.

6   BROUSSARD, Louis. "T. S. Eliot." See 20.2.

7   BROWN, Spencer. "T. S. Eliot's Latest Poetic Drama." *Commentary* 17(1954): 367–372. (A study of *The Confidential Clerk*.)

8   CARNE-ROSS, Donald. "The Position of 'The Family Reunion' in the Work of T. S. Eliot." *Revista di Letterature Moderne* 2(1950): 125–140.

9   DICKINSON, Donald H. "Mr. Eliot's *Hotel Universe*." See 26.3.

10 DREW, Elizabeth. *T. S. Eliot: The Design of His Poetry*. New York: Scribners, 1949. [34-Scribner.]

11 FERGUSON, Frances. "Action as Passion: *Tristan* and *Murder in the Cathedral*." *KR* 9(Spring, 1947): 201–221.

12 GALLUP, Donald. *T. S. Eliot: A Bibliography*. London: Faber and Faber, 1952. (A complete work up to 1952.)

13 GARDNER, Helen. *The Art of T. S. Eliot*. London: Cresset, 1949; New York: Dutton, 1959.

14 GARDNER, Helen. "The Comedies of T. S. Eliot." *SR* 74(1966): 153–175.

15 GASSNER, John. "T. S. Eliot: The Poet as Anti-Modernist." See 14.10.

16 GLICKSBERG, Charles I. "The Spirit of Irony in Eliot's Plays." *PrS* 29(1955): 222–237.

17 GREEN, E. J. H. *T. S. Eliot et la France*. Paris: Boivin, 1951.

18 HAMALIAN, Leo. "Mr. Eliot's Saturday Evening Service." *Accent* 10(1950): 195–206.

19 HÜBNER, Walter. "T. S. Eliot und das neue Drama." *Neuphilologische Zeitschrift* 5(1950): 337–352. (Analysis of *Murder in the Cathedral* with references to *Family Reunion*.)

20 INSERILLO, Charles R. "Wish and Desire: Two Poles of the Imagination in the Drama of Arthur Miller and T. S. Eliot." *XUS* 1(1962): 247–258. (Compares *Death of a Salesman* with *The Family Reunion*.)

21 JONES, David E. *The Plays of T. S. Eliot*. London: Routledge and Kegan Paul, 1960. (Very useful.)*

22 KAUL, R. K. "Rhyme and Blank Verse in Drama: A Note on Eliot." *ES* 15(1964): 96–99.

23 KENNEDY, Richard S. "Working Out Salvation with Diligence: The Plays of T. S. Eliot." *U Wichita Bul* 40(1964): 1–11.

1   KLINE, Peter. "The Spiritual Center of Eliot's Plays." *KR* 21(1959): 457–472.

2   KNIEGER, Bernard. "The Dramatic Achievement of T. S. Eliot." *MD* 3(1961): 387–392.

3   KRAMER, Hilton. "T. S. Eliot in New York." *WR* 14(1950): 303–305. (Critical review of *The Cocktail Party*.)

4   LAWLOR, John. "The Formal Achievement of *The Cocktail Party*." *VQR* 30(1954): 431–451.

5   LIGHTFOOT, Marjorie J. "Charting Eliot's Course in Drama." *ETJ* 20(1968): 186–207.

6   MAC LEISH, Archibald. "The Poet as Playwright." *Atlantic* 195(Feb., 1955): 49–52. (Contests Eliot's assumptions about verse drama and stage illusion.)

7   MATTHIESSEN, F. O. *The Achievement of T. S. Eliot*. 3d ed. with an additional chapter by C. L. Barber. New York: Oxford, 1958. (A valuable study.)*

8   MURRY, J. Middleton. "A Note on 'The Family Reunion'." *EIC* 1(1951): 67–73.

9   PALMER, Richard E. "Existentialism in T. S. Eliot's *The Family Reunion*." *MD* 5(1962): 174–186.

10 PETER, John. "Sin and Soda—*The Cocktail Party*." *Scrutiny* (England) 17(1950): 61–66.

11 PETER, John. "The Family Reunion." *Scrutiny* (England), 16(1949): 219–230.

12 ROBBINS, R. H. *The T. S. Eliot Myth*. New York: Schuman, 1951.

13 SCOTT, N. A., Jr. "T. S. Eliot's *The Cocktail Party*: Of Redemption and Vocation." *Religion in Life* 20(1951): 286–294.

14 SMIDT, Kristian. *Poetry and Belief in the Work of T. S. Eliot*. London: Routledge, 1961.

15 SMITH, Carol H. "Eliot as Playwright." *Nation* 203 (1966): 325–328.

16 SMITH, Carol H. *T. S. Eliot's Dramatic Theory and Practice*. Princeton: Princeton UP, 1963. (A useful study of Eliot's evolution of dramatic forms.)*

17 SMITH, Grover. "The Ghosts in T. S. Eliot's 'The Elder Statesman'." *N&Q* 7(1960): 233–235.

18 SMITH, Grover. *T. S. Eliot's Poetry and Plays: A Study in Sources and Meaning*. Chicago: U of Chicago P, 1956.

19 SPANOS, William V. "T. S. Eliot's *The Family Reunion*: The Strategy of Sacramental Transfiguration." *DramS*, 4(1964): 3–28.

20 SPEAIGHT, Robert. "With Becket in *Murder in the Cathedral*." *SR* 74(1966): 176–187.

21 STAMM, Rudolph. "The Orestes Theme in Three Plays by Eugene O'Neill, T. S. Eliot, and Jean-Paul Sartre." *ES* 30(1949), 244–255.

22 STELZMANN, Rainulf A. "The Theology of T. S. Eliot's Dramas." *XUS* 1(1961): 7–17.

23 TATE, Allen, ed. *T. S. Eliot: The Man and His Work*. New York: Delacorte Press, 1966. (Valuable essays by several authors.)*

1 UNGER, Leonard. *T. S. Eliot.* U of Minnesota Pamphlets, No. 8 Minneapolis: U of Minnesota P, 1961. (Brief but penetrating insights.)

2 WARD, Anne. "Speculations on Eliot's Time-World: An Analysis of *The Family Reunion* in Relation to Hulme and Bergson." *AL* 21(1949): 18–34.

3 WEISSTEIN, Ulrich. "Form as Content in the Drama of T. S. Eliot." *WR* 23(1959): 239–246.

4 WILLIAMSON, George. *A Reader's Guide to T. S. Eliot.* New Rork: Noonday Press, 1953. [N106]. (Informative introduction to Eliot's meaning and method.)*

5 WOOL, Sandra. "Weston Revisited." *Accent* 10(1950): 207–212. (Discusses *The Cocktail Party*.)

Fitch, Clyde (1865–1909)

6 *Plays by Clyde Fitch.* 4 vols. Ed. by Montrose J. Moses and Virginia Gerson. Boston: Little, Brown, 1915.

7 BROOKS, Van Wyck. "New York: UP-Town." *The Confident Years.* See 1.10.

8 BURTON, Richard. See 12.2.

9 CLARK, Barrett H. "Clyde Fitch." See 12.5.

10 MORRIS, Lloyd. See 2.2.

11 MOSES, Montrose J. "Concerning Clyde Fitch and the Local Sense." See 6.1.

12 MOSES, Montrose J., and Virginia GERSON. *Clyde Fitch and His Letters.* Boston: Little, Brown, 1924.

13 PHELPS, William Lyon. "Clyde Fitch." See 13.9.

14 QUINN, Arthur H. "Clyde Fitch and the Development of Social Comedy." See 6.3.

15 SIEVERS, W. David. "Clyde Fitch and Inherited Faculties." See 8.9.

Green, Paul (1894–)

16 GREEN, Paul. *Five Plays of the South.* New York: Hill and Wang, 1963. (Introduction by John Gassner emphasizes Green's humanitarian views.)

17 GREEN, Paul. *The House of Connelly and Other Plays.* New York: French, 1931.

18 ADAMS, Agatha Boyd. *Paul Green of Chapel Hill.* Chapel Hill: U of North Carolina P, 1951.*

19 BROWN, John Mason. "The Playwright and the American Theatre." See 12.1.

20 CARMER, Carl. "Paul Green: The Making of an American Dramatist." *TArts* 16(1932): 995–1006.

1 DUSENBURY, Winifred L. "In the South." See 21.11.

2 GAGEY, Edmond M. See 12.13.

3 GREEN, Paul. *Drama and the Weather: Some Notes and Papers on Life and the Theatre.* New York: French, 1958.

4 GREEN, Paul. *Dramatic Heritage.* New York: French, 1953.

5 ISAACS, E. J. R. "Paul Green—A Case in Point." *TArts* 25(1941): 489–498.

6 JONES, H. M. "Paul Green." *SWR* 14(1928): 1–8.

7 MANTLE, Burns. "Paul Green." See 13.1.

8 MANTLE, Burns. "Paul Green." See 13.2.

9 QUINN, Arthur H. "The Drama of the Provinces." See 6.3.

10 SIEVERS, W. David. "Paul Green." See 8.9.

Hellman, Lillian (1905–   )

11 HELLMAN, Lillian. *Six Plays.* New York: Modern Library, 1960.

12 ADLER, Jacob H. "Miss Hellman's Two Sisters." *ETJ* 15(1963): 112–117. (On *Toys in the Attic* and Chekov's *Three Sisters*.)

13 BEYER, William H. "Strindberg Heritage." See 21.6.

14 CLARK, B. H. "Lillian Hellman." *CE* 6(1944): 127–133.

15 DUSENBURY, Winifred L. "In the South." See 21.11.

16 GAGEY, Edmond M. See 12.13.

17 GASSNER, John. "Lillian Hellman: *The Autumn Garden*." See 14.9.

18 GOULD, Jean. "Lillian Hellman." See 14.13.

19 HELLMAN, Lillian. *An Unfinished Woman.* New York: Little, Brown, 1969. (Autobiography with frankness.)

20 ISAACS, E. J. R. "Lillian Hellman: A Playwright on the March." *TArts*, 28(1944): 19–24.

21 KRUTCH, Joseph W. See 12.20.

22 LEWIS, Allan. "The Survivors of the Depression—Hellman, Odets, Shaw." See 14.18.

23 NATHAN, George Jean. "Lillian Hellman." See 15.5.

24 SIEVERS, W. David. "Lillian Hellman." See 8.9.

25 TRIESCH, Manfred. *The Lillian Hellman Collection at the U of Texas.* Austin, Texas: U of Texas Humanities Research Center, 1966. (Full descriptions of manuscripts and other items.)

Herne, James A. (1839–1901)

26 *Shore Acres and Other Plays* by James A. Herne. Ed. by Mrs. James A. Herne New York: S. French, 1928.

1   *The Early Plays of James A. Herne*. Ed. by Arthur H. Quinn. Princeton, N.J.: Princeton UP, 1940.

2   EDWARDS, Herbert J., and Julie A. HERNE. *James A. Herne: The Rise of Realism in American Drama*. Orono: U of Maine Studies, 1964. (The best biographical study of Herne based on his daughter's notes.)*

3   HATLEN, Theodore. "Margaret Fleming and the Boston Independent Theater." *ETJ* 8(1956): 17–21.

4   HERNE, James A. "Act III of 'Griffith Davenport', with a Prefatory Note by Arthur Hobson Quinn and a Commentary by Julie A. Herne." *AL* 24(1952): 330–351.

5   MORTON, Frederick. "James A. Herne." *TArts* 24(1940): 899–902.

6   MOSES, Montrose J. "James A. Herne and the Realistic Drama." See 6.1.

7   PIZER, Donald. "An 1890 Account of Margaret Fleming." *AL* 27(1955): 264–267. (A review by Hamlin Garland.)

8   PIZER, Donald. "The Radical Drama in Boston, 1889–1891." *NEQ* 31(1958): 361–374.

9   QUINN, Arthur H. "Ibsen and Herne—Theory and Facts." *AL* 19(1947): 171–177.

10 QUINN, Arthur H. "James A. Herne and the Realism of Character." See 6.3.

11 WAGGONER, H. H. "The Growth of a Realist: James A. Herne." *NEQ* 15(1942): 62–73.

Howard, Sidney (1891–1939)

12 BACON, Leonard. "Appreciation." *SRL* 20(1939): 8.

13 BROWN, John Mason. "The Playwright and the American Theatre." See 12.1.

14 CLARK, Barrett H. "His Voice Was American." *TArts* 33(1949): 26–31.

15 CLARK, Barrett H. "Letters from Sidney Howard." *TArts* 25(1941): 276–286.

16 CLARK, Barrett H. "Sidney Howard: A Critical Appraisal of an Intensely Serious Playwright." *Theatre Guild Mag* 8(1930): 21–22, 25–26.

17 CLARK, Barrett H. "Sidney Howard." See 12.4.

18 DUSENBURY, Winifred L. "An Unhappy Family." See 21.11.

19 FLEXNER, Eleanor. "Sidney Howard." See 12.12.

20 ISAACS, Edith J. R. "Sidney Howard." *TArts* 23(1939): 723.

21 ISAACS, Edith J. R. "They Knew What They Wanted." *TArts* 23 (1939): 862.

22 ISAACS, Edith J. R. "Yellow Jack." *TArts* 18 (1934): 326.

1 KRUTCH, Joseph Wood. "The Dramatic Variety of Sidney Howard." *Nation* 137(1933): 294–295.

2 KRUTCH, Joseph Wood. "Three New Realists." See 12.20.

3 MANTLE, Burns. "Sidney Howard." See 13.1.

4 MANTLE, Burns. "Sidney Howard." See 13.2.

5 MESERVE, Walter J. "Sidney Howard and the Social Drama of the Twenties." *MD* 6(1963): 256–266.

6 QUINN, Arthur H. "The New Realism of Character." See 6.3.

7 SIEVERS, W. David. "Sidney Howard." See 8.9.

8 WILLIAMS, Herschel. "The Late Christopher Bean." *TArts* 17(1933): 18.

9 YOUNG, Stark. "Alien Corn." *New Republic* 74(1933): 101.

10 YOUNG, Stark. "Dodsworth." *New Republic* 78(1934): 134.

11 YOUNG, Stark. "Ned McCobb's Daughter." *New Republic* 40(1926): 20.

Inge, William (1913–   )

12 BRUSTEIN, Robert. "The Men-taming Women of William Inge." *Harper's* 217(1958): 52–57.

13 DOWNER, Alan. See 12.9.

14 DUSENBURY, Winifred L. "Personal Failure." See 21.11.

15 *Four Plays by William Inge.* New York: Random, 1958.

16 GASSNER, John. "William Inge and the Subtragic Muse." See 14.9.

17 GOULD, Jean. "William Inge." See 14.13.

18 GROVES, Gerald. "The Success of William Inge." *Critic* 23(1964–65): 16–19.

19 HERRON, Ima H. "Our Vanishing Towns: Modern Broadway Versions." *SWR* 51(1966): 209–220. (Treats the plays of William Inge.)

20 LEWIS, Allan. "The Emergent Deans—Kingsley, Inge and Company." See 14.18.

21 MILLSTEIN, Gilbert. "The Dark at the Top of William Inge." *Esquire* 50(1958): 60–63.

22 NATHAN, George Jean. "William Inge." See 15.5.

23 SHUMAN, R. Baird. *William Inge.* New York: Twayne, 1965. (Detailed accounts of plots.)

24 SIEVERS, W. David. "William Inge." See 8.9.

25 WEALES, Gerald. See 10.5.

26 WOLFSON, Lester M. "Inge, O'Neill, and the Human Condition." *Southern Speech Journal* 22(1957): 221–232.

Kaufman, George S. (1889–1961)

1 CARMER, Carl. "George Kaufman—Playmaker to Broadway." *TArts* 16(1932): 807–815.

2 CORBIN, John. "George Kaufman." *SRL* 9(1933): 385–386. (Analysis of *Of Thee I Sing*.)

3 DICKINSON, Thomas H. "Modern Domestic Comedy: Kaufman and Connelly." See 12.8.

4 FLEXNER, Eleanor. "George S. Kaufman." See 12.12.

5 FREEDLEY, George. "George S. Kaufman: 1889–1962." *MD* 6(1963): 241–244.

6 GAGEY, Edmond M. See 12.13.

7 GOULD, Jean. "George S. Kaufman and Moss Hart." See 14.13.

8 HART, Moss. *Act One: An Autobiography*. New York: Random, 1959. (Interesting account of collaboration with Kaufman.)

9 KAUFMAN, George S. "Music to My Ears." *Stage* 15(1938): 27–30. (The playwright discusses collaboration.)

10 KRUTCH, Joseph W. "Comedy." See 12.20.

11 KRUTCH, Joseph W. "The Random Satire of George S. Kaufman." *Nation* 137(1938): 156–158.

12 MANTLE, Burns. "George S. Kaufman." See 13.1.

13 MANTLE, Burns. "George Kaufman, Moss Hart." See 13.2.

14 MERSAND, Joseph. "George S. Kaufman: Master of Technique." See 13.3.

15 MOSES, Montrose J. "George S. Kaufman: A Satirist in the American Theatre." *North Am Rev* 237(1934): 76–83. (Emphasis on seriousness of the playwright.)

16 NATHAN, George Jean. "George S. Kaufman." See 15.5.

17 QUINN, Arthur H. "The New Realism of Character." See 6.3.

Kingsley, Sidney (1906–   )

18 COUSINS, Norman. "Jefferson and Hamilton." *SRL* 26(1943): 26, 45.

19 DUSENBURY, Winifred L. "The Lonely Hero." See 21.11.

20 GAGEY, Edmond M. See 12.13.

21 GASSNER, John. "Jefferson and Hamilton in Drama." *Current History* n.s., 4(1943): 88–91.

22 GILDER, Rosamond. "Patriots, 1776, 1943." *TArts* 27(1943): 201–204.

23 LEWIS, Allan. "The Emergent Deans—Kingsley, Inge and Company." See 14.18.

24 NATHAN, George Jean. "The Best Play of the Season." *American Mercury* 56(1943): 486–487.

25 SIEVERS, W. David. "Two Naturalists—Kingsley and Hecht." See 8.9.

26 YOUNG, Stark. "Dead End." *New Republic* 85(1935): 21.

MacLeish, Archibald (1892–   )

1   BOND, Charles M. "*J. B. Is Not Job.*" *BuR* 9(1961): 272–280.

2   BROUSSARD, Louis. "Archibald MacLeish." See 20.2.

3   D'ARCY, Martin C. "*J. B.*, Wrong Answer to the Problem of Evil." *Cath W* 190(1959): 81–85.

4   FALK, Signi. *Archibald MacLeish*. New York: Twayne, 1965. (Treats the dramas.)

5   GREBSTEIN, Sheldon. "*J B* and the Problem of Evil." *UKCR* 29(1963): 253–261.

6   KRUTCH, Joseph W. "The Poetic Drama." See 12.20.

7   KRUTCH, Joseph W. "The Universe at Stage Center." *TArts* 42(1959): 9–11.

8   LEWIS, Allan. "Man's Relation to God—MacLeish and Chayefsky." See 14.18.

9   SICKELS, Eleanor M. "MacLeish and the Fortunate Fall." *AL* 35(1963): 205–217. (Discusses *J. B.*)

10   VANN, J. Don. "MacLeish's *J. B.*" *Am N&Q* 2(1964): 150.

11   WEINER, Herbert. "Job on Broadway." *Commentary* 26(1958): 153–158.

12   WHITE, Jean. "Will to Live Is Key to MacLeish's 'J. B.'" *LJ* 84(1959): 36–37.

Miller, Arthur (1915–   )

13   MILLER, Arthur. *Collected Plays*. New York: Viking, 1957. (Contains prefatory comment by the playwright.)

14   ALLSOP, Kenneth. "A Conversation with Arthur Miller." *Encounter* 8(1959): 58–60.

15   BARKSDALE, Richard K. "Social Background in the Plays of Miller and Williams." *CLAJ* 6(1963): 161–169.

16   BENTLEY, Eric. "Miller's Innocence." *New Rep* 128(1953): 22–23. (Criticism of *The Crucible* as close to melodrama.)

17   BLOCK, Haskell, and Robert G. SHEDD. "Arthur Miller." See 13.20.

18   BRANDON, Henry. "The State of the Theatre: A Conversation with Arthur Miller." *Harper's* 221(1960): 63–69.

19   BRASHEAR, William R. "The Empty Bench: Morality, Tragedy and Arthur Miller." *MQR* 5(1966): 270–278.

20   BROUSSARD, Louis. "Arthur Miller." See 20.2.

21   BROWN, Ivor. "As London Sees Willy Loman." *NY Times Mag*, August 28, 1949, pp. 1, 59.

22   BRUSTEIN, Robert. "The Memory of Heroism." *TDR* 4(1960): 3–9.

1 CASSELL, Richard A. "Arthur Miller's 'Rage of Conscience'." *Ball State Teachers Col Forum* 1(1960–61): 31–36.

2 CLARK, Eleanor. "Old Glamour, New Gloom." *PR* 16(1949): 631–636. (Criticizes *Death of a Salesman*.)

3 DE SCHWEINITZ, George. "*Death of a Salesman:* A Note on Epic and Tragedy." *WHR* 14(1960): 91–96.

4 DILLINGHAM, William B. "Arthur Miller and the Loss of Conscience." *EUQ* 16(1960): 40–50.

5 DOWNER, Alan S. "The Two Worlds of Arthur Miller and Tennessee Williams." *Princeton Alumni Wk* 52(1961): 8–11, **17,** 20.

6 DRIVER, Tom. "Strength and Weakness in Arthur Miller." *TDR* 4(1960): 45–52.

7 DUSENBURY, Winifred L. "Personal Failure." See 21.11.

8 EISSENSTAT, Martha T. "Arthur Miller: A Bibliography." *MD* 5(1962): 93–106.

9 EPSTEIN, Arthur D. "A Look at *A View from the Bridge.*" *TSLL* 7(1965): 109–122.

10 FULLER, A. Howard. "A Salesman In Everybody." *Fortune* 39(1949): 79–80.

11 GANZ, Arthur. "Arthur Miller: After the Silence." *DramS* 3(1964): 520–530.

12 GANZ, Arthur. "The Silence of Arthur Miller." *DramS* 3(1963): 224–237.

13 GASSNER, John. "New American Playwrights: Williams, Miller, and Others." See 14.10.*

14 GOULD, Jean. "Arthur Miller." See 14.13.

15 HOGAN, Robert. *Arthur Miller.* U of Minnesota Pamphlets No 40, Minneapolis: U of Minnesota P, 1964. (A helpful introduction.)*

16 HUFTEL, Sheila. *Arthur Miller: The Burning Glass.* New York: Citadel, 1965. (An enthusiastic appraisal of Miller's plays.)

17 HYNES, Joseph A. "Attention Must Be Paid. . . ." *CE* 23(1962): 574–578. (On *Death of a Salesman*.)

18 JACKSON, Esther M. "*Death of a Salesman:* Tragic Myth in the Modern Theater." *CLAJ* 7(1963): 63–76.

19 KENNEDY, Sighle. "Who Killed the Salesman." *CathW* 171(1950): 110–116.

20 LAWRENCE, Stephen A. "The Right Dream in Miller's *Death of a Salesman.*" *CE* 25(1964): 547–549.

21 LEWIS, Allan. "Arthur Miller—Return to the Self." See 14.18.

22 LOUGHLIN, Richard L. "Tradition and Tragedy in 'All My Sons'." *English Review*, 14(1964): 23–27.

23 MAULNIER, Thierry. Les Sorcières de Salem d'Arthur Miller." *Revue de Paris*, 52(1955): 137–149. (On *The Crucible*.)

24 MC ANANY, Emile G. "The Tragic Commitment: Some Notes on Arthur Miller." *MD* 5(1962): 11–20.

25 MC CARTHY, Mary. "Naming Names: The Arthur Miller Case." *Encounter* 8(1957): 23–25.

1 MILLER, Arthur. "Arthur Miller Talks: The Contemporary Theater." *MQR* 6(1967): 153–163.

2 MILLER, Arthur. "The Family in Modern Drama." *Atlantic* 197(1956): 35–41.

3 MILLER, Arthur. "Morality and Modern Drama." *ETJ* 10(1958): 190–202. (Miller comments on his own work and that of Eliot and Williams.)

4 MILLER, Arthur. "The Playwright and the Atomic World." *ColQ* 5(1956): 117–137.

5 MILLER, Arthur. "Tragedy and the Common Man." *TA* 35(1951): 48–50.

6 MILLER, Arthur, and Gore VIDAL, et al. "Death of a Salesman, a Symposium." *TDR* 2(1958): 63–69. (A program presented by the University of Minnesota radio station.)

7 MOSS, Leonard. "Biographical and Literary Allusion in *After the Fall*." *ETJ* 18(1966): 34–40.

8 NATHAN, George Jean. "Arthur Miller." See 15.5.

9 NEWMAN, William J. "The Plays of Arthur Miller." *TC* 144(1958): 491–496.

10 PARKER, Brian. "Point of View in Arthur Miller's *Death of a Salesman*." *UTQ* 35(1966): 144–157.

11 POPKIN, Henry. "Arthur Miller: The Strange Encounter." *SR* 68(1960): 34–60.

12 PRUDHOE, John. "Arthur Miller and the Tradition of Tragedy." *ES* 43(1962): 430–439.

13 ROSENFIELD, John. "Inhibitions of the Postwar Reaction." *SWR* 38(1953): 347–350. (Praise of Miller's *Death of a Salesman* and questions as to its not greater success.)

14 ROUERE, Richard H. "Arthur Miller's Conscience." *New Republic* 136(1957): 13–15.

15 SCHNEIDER, Daniel E. "Play of Dreams." *TArts* 33(1949): 18–21. (A psychiatric analysis of *Death of a Salesman*.)

16 SCHNEIDER, Daniel E. *The Psychoanalyst and the Artist*. New York: Farrar, Straus, 1950. (Provides helpful insight.)

17 SEAGER, Allan. "The Creative Agony of Arthur Miller." *Esquire* 52(1959): 123–126.

18 SHEA, Albert A. "Death of a Salesman." *Canadian Forum* 29(1949): 86–87. (The play exposes the values of our present society.)

19 SIEGEL, Paul N. "Willy Loman and King Lear." *CE* 17(1956): 341–345.

20 SIEVERS, W. David. "Tennessee Williams and Arthur Miller." See 8.9.

21 STEINBERG, M. W. "Arthur Miller and the Idea of Modern Tragedy." *DR* 40(1960): 329–340.

22 TYNAN, Kenneth. "American Blues: The Plays of Arthur Miller and Tennessee Williams." *Encounter* (London) 2(1954): 13–19.

23 WALKER, Philip. "Arthur Miller's *The Crucible:* Tragedy or Allegory?" *Western Speech* 20(1956): 222–224.

1 WARSHOW, Robert. "The Liberal Conscience in *The Crucible*." *Commentary* 15(1953): 265–271.

2 WEALES, Gerald. "Arthur Miller." See 10.5.

3 WEALES, Gerald, ed. *Arthur Miller: 'Death of a Salesman': Text and Criticism*. New York: Viking Press, 1967. [VCL2] (Contains criticism by various authors.)*

4 WEALES, Gerald. "Arthur Miller: Man and His Image." *TDR* 7(1962): 165–180.

5 WELLAND, Dennis. *Arthur Miller*. New York: Grove, 1961. (Brief sketch of Miller's intentions.)

6 WIEGAND, William. "Arthur Miller and the Man Who Knows." *WR* 21(1957): 85–103. (Treats all of Miller's published work.)

7 WILLIAMS, Raymond. "The Realism of Arthur Miller." *CritQ* 1(1959): 140–149.

8 YORKS, Samuel A. "Joe Keller and His Sons." *WHR* 13(1959): 401–407.

Moody, William Vaughn (1869–1910)

9 DICKINSON, Thomas H. "Playwright as Poet: William Vaughn Moody." See 12.8.

10 HALPERN, Martin. *William Vaughn Moody*. New York: Twayne, 1964. (Valuable interpretation and criticism of Moody's plays.)*

11 HENRY, David W. *William Vaughn Moody: A Study*. Boston: Humphries, 1934. (Contains twenty new letters.)

12 LOVETT, Robert M. "Memories of William Vaughn Moody." *Atlantic* 147(1931): 385–393.

13 MACKAYE, Percy, ed. *Letters to Harriet*. Boston: Houghton Mifflin, 1935. (Letters from Moody to his wife, 1901–1909.)

14 *The Poems and Plays of William Vaughn Moody*. Introduction by John M. Manley. 2 vols. Boston and New York: Houghton Mifflin, 1912.

15 QUINN, Arthur H. "William Vaughn Moody and the Drama of Revolt." See 6.3.

16 RIGGS, Thomas, Jr. "Prometheus 1900." *AL* 22(1951): 399–423.

Odets, Clifford (1906–1963)

17 ODETS, Clifford. *Six Plays*. New York: Modern Library, 1939.

18 BLOCK, Haskell, and Robert G. SHEDD. "Clifford Odets." See 13.20.

19 BROWN, John Mason. "America's Yield." See 15.15.

20 BROWN, John Mason. "Mr. Odet's Return." See 15.14.

21 BROWN, John Mason. "Sing Me a Song with Social Significance." See 11.19.

22 CLURMAN, Harold. See 9.2.

1 DUSENBURY, Winifred L. "Night Music." See 21.11.

2 GASSNER, John. "Clifford Odets." See 14.10.

3 GASSNER, John. "The Long Journey of Talent." *TArts* 33(1949): 25–30. (Odets' "subjective perversity.")

4 GOULD, Jean. "Clifford Odets." See 14.13.

5 HUNT, Albert. "Only Soft-Centered Left: Odets and Social Theatre." *Encore* 8(1961): 5–12.

6 ISAACS, E. J. R. "Clifford Odets." *TArts* 23(1939): 257–264.

7 LEWIS, Allan. "The Survivors of the Depression—Hellman, Odets, Shaw." See 14.18.

8 MANTLE, Burns. "Clifford Odets." See 13.2.

9 MENDELSOHN, Michael J. "Clifford Odets and the American Family." *DramS* 3(1963): 238–243.

10 MERSAND, Joseph. "Clifford Odets: Dramatist of Young America." See 13.3.

11 NATHAN, George Jean. "Clifford Odets." See 15.5.

12 ODETS, Clifford. "How a Playwright Triumphs." *Harper's* 233(1966): 64–74.

13 RABKIN, Gerald. "The Road from Marxist Commitment: Clifford Odets." See 8.15.

14 SHUMAN, R. Baird. *Clifford Odets*. New York: Twayne, 1962. (Good critical analysis.)*

15 SIEVERS, W. David. "Clifford Odets." See 8.9.

16 YOUNG, Stark. "Convertible Top." *New Republic* 84(1935): 190. (Praises *Waiting for Lefty*.)

O'Neill, Eugene (1888–1953)

17 ABEL, Lionel. "O'Neill and His Critics." *New Leader* 61(1958): 25–26.

18 ALEXANDER, Doris M. "Captain Brant and Captain Brassbound: The Origin of an O'Neill Character." *MLN* 74(1959): 306–310.

19 ALEXANDER, Doris M. "Eugene O'Neill and Charles Lever." *MD* 5(1963): 415–420. (Lever's *Charles O'Malley, The Irish Dragoon* was an important source for *A Touch of the Poet*.)

20 ALEXANDER, Doris M. "Eugene O'Neill as Social Critic." *AQ* 6(1954): 349–363. (*The Hairy Ape, Marco Millions, The Great God Brown, Servitude,* and *Days Without End* as criticism of American society.)

21 ALEXANDER, Doris M. "Eugene O'Neill, 'The Hound of Heaven,' and the 'Hell Hole'." *MLQ* 20(1959): 307–314.

22 ALEXANDER, Doris M. "Hugo of *The Iceman Cometh:* Realism in O'Neill." *AQ* 5(1953): 357–366. [The character of Hugo is based on Hippolyte Havel of the Provincetown group.]

23 ALEXANDER, Doris M. "*Lazarus Laughed* and Buddha." *MLQ* 17(1956): 357–365.

1 ALEXANDER, Doris M. "Psychological Fate in *Mourning Becomes Electra*." PMLA 68(1953): 923–934.*

2 ALEXANDER, Doris M. "*Strange Interlude* and Schopenhauer." *AL* 25(1953): 213–228.

3 ALEXANDER, Doris M. *The Tempering of Eugene O'Neill*. New York: Harcourt, Brace & World, 1962. (Treats O'Neill's early years up to *Beyond the Horizon*.)

4 ANDERSON, John. "Eugene O'Neill." *TArts* 15(1931): 938–942.

5 ANDREACH, Robert J. "O'Neill's Women in *The Iceman Cometh*." *Renascence* 18(1966): 89–98.

6 ARESTAD, Sverre. "*The Iceman Cometh* and *The Wild Duck*." *SS* 20(1948): 1–11.

7 ASSELINEAU, Roger. "*Mourning Becomes Electra* as a Tragedy." *MD* 1(1958): 143–150.

8 BAKER, George Pierce. "O'Neill's First Decade." *YR* 15(1926), 789–792.

9 BASSO, Hamilton. "The Tragic Sense." *NY* 24(Feb. 28, March 6, March 13, 1948): 34–38, 40, 42–43; 34–38, 40, 43–44, 46–47; 37–40, 42, 44, 47. (Biography and sound criticism.)

10 BENTLEY, Eric. "The Return of Eugene O'Neill." *Atlantic Monthly* 178(1946): 64–66.

11 BENTLEY, Eric. "Trying to Like O'Neill." *KR* 14(1952): 476–92. (Sees O'Neill's chief weakness as "ambition to transcend realism.")

12 BERKELMAN, Robert. "O'Neill's Everyman." *SAQ* 58(1959): 609–616. (Analysis of *The Great God Brown*.)

13 BJORK, Lennart A. "The Swedish Critical Reception of O'Neill's Posthumous Plays." *SS* 38(1966): 231–250.

14 BLACKBURN, Clara. "Continental Influences on Eugene O'Neill's Expressionistic Dramas." *AL* 13(1941): 103–133.

15 BOULTON, Agnes. *Part of a Long Story*. New York: Doubleday, 1958. (An account of O'Neill by his second wife.)

16 BOWEN, Croswell. *The Curse of the Misbegotten*. New York: McGraw-Hill, 1959. (O'Neill's family life as seen by his second son, Shane.)

17 BRASHEAR, William R. "The Wisdom of Silenus in O'Neill's 'Iceman.' " *AL* 36(1964): 180–188.

18 BROUSSARD, Louis. "Eugene O'Neill." See 20.2.

19 BROWN, John Mason. "Eugene O'Neill: 1888–1953." *SatR*, 36(1953), 26–28. (An appraisal by an important critic.)

20 BRUSTEIN, Robert. *The Theatre of Revolt*. Boston: Little, Brown, 1964. (Treats O'Neill and the dilemma of modern man in a world without God.)

21 BRYER, Jackson R. "Forty Years of O'Neill Criticism: A Selected Bibliography." *MD* 4(1961): 196–216.

22 CARGILL, Oscar, N. Bryllion FAGIN, and William J. FISHER, eds. *O'Neill and His Plays: Four Decades of Criticism*. New York: New York UP, 1961. [NYU Pr.] (A useful collection of biographical and critical essays, including letters by O'Neill.)*

1 CARPENTER, Frederic I. *Eugene O'Neill*. New York: Twayne, 1964. (Biographical account and a study of twenty of O'Neill's plays.)

2 CARPENTER, Frederick I. "The Romantic Tragedy of Eugene O'Neill." *CE* 6(1945): 250–258.

3 CERF, Walter. "Psychoanalysis and the Realistic Drama." *JAAC* 16(1958): 328–336. (Compares *Long Day's Journey* with Arthur Laurent's *A Clearing in the Woods*.)

4 CESTRE, Charles. "Eugene O'Neill." *EA* 1(1937): 93–94.

5 CHABROWE, Leonard. "Dionysus in *The Iceman Cometh*." *MD* 4(1962): 377–388.

6 CLARK, Barrett H. "Aeschylus and O'Neill." *EJ* 21(1932): 699–710.

7 CLARK, Barrett H. *Eugene O'Neill: The Man and His Plays*. New York: Dover, 1947.

8 CONLIN, Matthew T. "The Tragic Effect in *Autumn Fire* and *Desire Under the Elms*." *MD* 1(1959): 228–235.

9 CORBIN, John. "O'Neill and Aeschylus." *SRL* 8(1932): 693–695.

10 DAICHES, David. "Mourning Becomes O'Neill." *Encounter* 16(1961): 74–78. (O'Neill's plays in the light of his son's disclosures.)

11 DAVIDSON, L. J. "Lazarus in Modern Literature." *EJ* 18(1929): 16–23.

12 DAY, Cyrus. "The Iceman and the Bridegroom: Some Observations on the Death of O'Neill's Salesman." *MD* 1(1958): 3–9.

13 DE VOTO, Bernard. "Minority Report." *SRL* 15(1936): 34. (Sees O'Neill as less than a first-rank author.)

14 DICKINSON, Hugh. "Eugene O'Neill: Fate as Form." *Drama Critique* 10(1967): 78–85.

15 DIRVANA, Nesterin. "Théatre Pur et Rythme Biologique." *Dialogues* (Istanbul) 1(1949): 87–105. (Structure and meaning of *Strange Interlude*.)

16 DOBREE, Bonamy. "Mr. O'Neill's Latest Play." *SR* 56(1948): 118–126. (Discussion of *The Iceman Cometh*.)

17 DOWNER, Alan S. "Eugene O'Neill as Poet of the Theater." *TArts* 35(1951): 22–23.

18 DOWNER, Alan S. "Tragedy and 'The Pursuit of Happiness': *Long Day's Journey Into Night*." *JA* 6(1961): 115–121.

19 DRIVER, Tom F. "On the Late Plays of Eugene O'Neill." *TDR* 3(1958): 8–20.

20 DUKES, Ashley. "The English Scene: O'Neill Succeeds." *TArts* 22(1938): 101–107.

21 EATON, Walter P. "Eugene O'Neill." *TArts* 4(1920): 286–289.

22 EATON, Walter P. "The Eugene O'Neill Collection." *Yale U Lib Gaz* 18(1943): 5–8.

23 EATON, Walter P. "O'Neill: New Risen Attic Stream." *ASch* 6(1937): 304–312.

24 EDEL, Leon. "Eugene O'Neill: The Face and the Mask." *UTQ* 7(1937): 18–34.*

1 ENGEL, Edwin A. "Eugene O'Neill's Long Day's Journey into Light." *MAQR* 63(1957): 348–354.

2 ENGEL, Edwin A. *The Haunted Heroes of Eugene O'Neill*. Cambridge, Mass.: Harvard UP, 1953. (A full-length study of O'Neill's plays.)*

3 ENGEL, Edwin A., et al. "O'Neill Issue." *MD* 3(1960): 219–332. (Fourteen articles on various aspects of O'Neill's work.)

4 FAGIN, N. Bryllion. "Eugene O'Neill." *AR* 16(1954): 14–26. (O'Neill's powerful dramatization of man's pain and perplexity.)

5 FALK, Doris V. *Eugene O'Neill and the Tragic Tension*. New Brunswick, N.J.: Rutgers UP, 1958.*

6 FALK, Doris V. "That Paradox, O'Neill." *MD* 6(1963): 221–238. (Shows blending of the vulgar with herioc and relates Denman Thompson's *The Old Homestead* to *Desire Under the Elms*.)

7 FERGUSON, Francis. "Eugene O'Neill." *Hound and Horn* 3(1930): 145–160.

8 FREEDMAN, Morris. "O'Neill and Contemporary American Drama." *CE* 23(1962): 570–574.

9 FRENZ, Horst. "Eugene O'Neill in Russia." *Poet Lore* 69(1943): 241–247.

10 FRENZ, Horst. "Eugene O'Neill in France." *Books Abroad* 19(1944), 140–141.

11 FRENZ, Horst. "Eugene O'Neill's Plays Printed Abroad." *CE* 5(1944): 340–341.

12 FRENZ, Horst, and Martin MUELLER. "More Shakespeare and Less Aeschylus in Eugene O'Neill's *Mourning Becomes Electra*." *AL* 38(1966): 85–100. (Traces the influence of Hamlet on O'Neill's trilogy.)

13 GASSNER, John. *Eugene O'Neill*. Univ. of Minnesota Pamphlets. Minneapolis: U of Minnesota P, 1965. [MPAW45.] (Good critical analysis.)

14 GASSNER, John. "Eugene O'Neill: The Course of a Major Dramatist." See 14.9.

15 GASSNER, John. "The Influence of Strindberg in the United States." *World Theatre* 11(1962): 21–29. (Treats the work of O'Neill and Williams.)

16 GASSNER, John. "O'Neill in Our Time." See 14.10.

17 GASSNER, John (ed.). *O'Neill: A Collection of Critical Essays*. Englewood Cliffs, N.J.: Prentice-Hall, 1964. [STC39.]

18 GEDDES, Virgil. *The Melodramadness of Eugene O'Neill*. Brookefield, Conn.: Brookfield Players, 1934.

19 GEIER, Woodrow. "O'Neill's Miracle Play." *Religion in Life* 16(1947): 515–526. (*Days Without End* and its Christian solution.)

20 GELB, Arthur, and Barbara. *O'Neill*. New York: Harper, 1962. [6629LE-Dell.] (Indispensable.)*

21 GLICKSBERG, Charles I. "The Modern Playwright and the Absolute." *QQ* 65(1958): 459–471. (Refers to O'Neill and Williams.)

22 GOULD, Jean. "Eugene O'Neill." See 14.13.

1   GRANGER, Bruce I. "Illusion and Reality in Eugene O'Neill." *MLN* 73(1958): 179–186.

2   HARTMAN, Murray. "*Desire Under the Elms* in the Light of Strindberg's Influence." *AL* 33(1961): 360–369.

3   HAYES, Richard. "Eugene O'Neill: The Tragic in Exile." *TArts* 47(1963): 68–69.

4   HAYWARD, I. N. "Strindberg's Influence on Eugene O'Neill." *Poet Lore* 29(1928): 596–604.

5   HERBERT, Edward. "Eugene O'Neill: An Evaluation by Fellow Playwrights." *MD* 6(1963): 239–240.

6   HOPKINS, Vivian C. " 'The Iceman' Seen Through 'The Lower Depths'." *CE* 11(1949): 81–87. (Compares O'Neill unfavorably with Gorky.)

7   HUGHES, Catharine R. "Eugene O'Neill: The Great Influence on American Theater." *Critic* 22(1963): 49–51.

8   ISAACS, Edith J. R. "Meet Eugene O'Neill." *TArts* 30(1946): 576–587.

9   KEMP, Harry. "Out of Provincetown—A Memoir of Eugene O'Neill." *Theatre Magazine* 51(1930): 22–23, 66.

10 KIRCHNER, Gustav. "Eugene O'Neill: The Iceman Cometh." *Neuphilologische Zeitschrift* 1(1950): 28–37.

11 KRUTCH, Joseph W. "Domestic Drama with Some Difference." *TArts* 40(1956): 25, 89–91.

12 KRUTCH, Joseph W. "Eugene O'Neill." See 2.6.

13 KRUTCH, Joseph W. "Eugene O'Neill, the Lonely Revolutionary." *TArts* 36(1952): 29–30, 78. (O'Neill rejected the ideals of his own times.)

14 KRUTCH, Joseph W. "Eugene O'Neill's Claim to Greatness." *NYTBR*, Chap. 22, 1957, pp. 1, 42.

15 KRUTCH, Joseph W. "Tragedy: Eugene O'Neill." See 12.20.

16 LAMM, Martin. "Problem Eugene O'Neill." *Bonniers Litterära Magasin* (Stockholm) 16(1947): 633–639.

17 *The Later Plays of Eugene O'Neill.* Ed. by Travis Bogard. New York: Random, 1966. [T91-Mod. Lib.]

18 LECKY, Eleazer. "*Ghosts* and *Mourning Becomes Electra:* Two Versions of Fate." *ArQ* 13(1957): 320–338.

19 LEECH, Clifford. *Eugene O'Neill.* New York: Grove, 1963. (General commentary; treats O'Neill's expressionism.)

20 LEWIS, Allan. "Eugene O'Neill—The Tragic Homecoming." See 14.18.

21 LOWELL, John, Jr. "Eugene O'Neill's Darker Brother." *TArts* 32(1948): 45–48. (Negroes in O'Neill's dramas.)

22 MACGOWAN, Kenneth. "O'Neill and a Mature Hollywood Outlook." *TArts* 42(1958): 79–81. (The film of *Desire Under the Elms.*)

23 MARCUS, Mordecai. "Eugene O'Neill's Debt to Thoreau in *A Touch of the Poet.*" *JEGP* 62(1963): 270–279. (Presents Hugh Quoil of *Walden* as a source for Major Melody.)

24 MILLER, Jordan Y. *Eugene O'Neill and the American Critics.* Hamden, Conn.: Archon, 1962. (Bibliography and collection of reviews.)

1 MILLER, Jordan Y. "The Georgia Plays of Eugene O'Neill." *GaR* 12(1958): 278–290.

2 MOTTRAM, Eric. "Men and Gods: A Study of Eugene O'Neill." *Encore* 10(1963): 26–44. (On a London production of *Hughie*.)

3 MUCHNIC, Helen. "Circe's Swine: Plays by Gorky and O'Neill." *Comparative Literature* 3(1951): 119–128. (Compares *The Lower Depths* with *The Iceman Cometh*.)

4 NATHAN, George Jean. "O'Neill: A Critical Summation." *American Mercury* 63(1946): 713–719.

5 NATHAN, George Jean. "O'Neill." See 13.7.

6 NATHAN, George Jean. *The Intimate Notebooks of George Jean Nathan*. New York: Knopf, 1932.

7 NICOLL, Allardyce. *World Drama from Aeschylus to Anouilh*. New York: Harcourt, Brace, 1950.

8 *Nine Plays* by Eugene O'Neill. Selected by the author. Foreword by Joseph Wood Krutch. New York: Liveright, 1932. (Now published by Random House.)

9 NORWOOD, Gilbert. "The Art of Eugene O'Neill." *DR* 21(1941): 143–157.

10 O'NEILL, Joseph P. "The Tragic Theory of Eugene O'Neill." *TSLL* 4(1963): 481–498. (Shows O'Neill's method in *Mourning Becomes Electra*.)

11 "The Ordeal of Eugene O'Neill." *Time* 48(Oct. 21, 1946): 71–78.

12 PALLETTE, Drew B. "O'Neill's *A Touch of the Poet* and His Other Last Plays." *ArQ* 13(1957): 308–319.

13 PARKS, Edd Winfield. "Eugene O'Neill's Quest." *TDR* 4(1960): 99–107.

14 PARKS, Edd Winfield. "Eugene O'Neill's Symbolism." *SR* 43(1935): 436–450.

15 PERRY, William. "Does the Buskin Fit O'Neill?" *UKCR* 15(1949): 281–287. (Examines O'Neill's concept of tragedy.)

16 *The Plays of Eugene O'Neill*. 3 vols. New York: Random, 1955.

17 POMMER, Henry F. "The Mysticism of *Lazarus Laughed*." *Crane Review* 8(1966): 83–91.

18 QUINN, Arthur H. "Eugene O'Neill, Poet and Mystic." *Scribners* 80(1926): 368–372.

19 QUINN, Arthur H. "Eugene O'Neill, Poet and Mystic." See 6.3.*

20 RACEY, Edgar F., Jr. "Myth as Tragic Structure in *Desire Under the Elms*." *MD* 5(1962): 42–46.

21 RALEIGH, John H. "O'Neill's *Long Day's Journey into Night* and New England Irish-Catholicism." *PR* 26(1959): 573–592.

22 RALEIGH, John H. *The Plays of Eugene O'Neill*. Carbondale: Southern Illinois UP, 1965. (Treats the literary qualities of O'Neill's plays, apart from the stage.)

1   REDFORD, Grant H. "Dramatic Art vs. Autobiography: A Long Look at *Long Day's Journey into Night.*" *CE* 25(1964): 527–535.

2   RUST, R. Dilworth. "The Unity of O'Neill's *S. S. Glencairn.*" *AL* 37(1965): 280–290. (Demonstrates that four one-act plays unite to form a cycle play.)

3   SALEM, James M. "Eugene O'Neill and the Sacrament of Marriage." *Serif* 3(1966): 23–25.

4   SANBORN, Ralph, and Barrett H. CLARK. *A Bibliography of the Works of Eugene O'Neill.* New York: Random, 1931. (Out of date, but still helpful.)

5   SAYLER, Oliver M. "Eugene O'Neill: Master of Naturalism." *Drama* 11(1921): 189–190.

6   SCHELLING, Felix E. *Appraisements and Asperities as to Some Contemporary Writers.* Philadelphia: Lippincott, 1922. (Treats *The Emperor Jones.*)

7   SHIPLEY, Joseph T. *The Art of Eugene O'Neill.* Seattle: U of Washington Book Store, 1928.

8   SIEVERS, W. David. "Freud, Jung, and O'Neill." See 8.9.

9   SKINNER, Richard Dana. *Eugene O'Neill: A Poet's Quest.* New York: Longmans, Green, 1935.

10 SKINNER, Richard Dana. "O'Neill—The Poet's Quest." *North American Review* 240(1935): 54–67.

11 STAFFORD, John. "Mourning Becomes America." *TSLL* 3(1963): 549–556. (On *Mourning Becomes Electra.*)

12 STAMM, Rudolf. "The Dramatic Experiments of Eugene O'Neill." *ES* 28(1947): 1–15.

13 STAMM, Rudolf. "A New Play by Eugene O'Neill." *ES* 29(1948): 138–145.

14 STAMM, Rudolf. See 30.21.

15 TAYLOR, Walter Fuller. "The Rise of Drama: Eugene O'Neill." See 2.7.

16 *Ten "Lost" Plays* by Eugene O'Neill. New York: Random, 1964.

17 THORP, Willard. "Dramatic Interlude, 1915–1940." See 2.8.

18 TRILLING, Lionel. "Eugene O'Neill." *New Republic* 88(1936): 176–178. (Traces the religious strain from *Fog* through *Days Without End.*)

19 VENA, Gary A. "The Role of the Prostitute in the Plays of Eugene O'Neill." *Drama Critique* 10(1967): 129–137: 11(1968): 9–14, 82–88.

20 VOWLES, Richard B. "Psychology and Drama: A Selected Checklist." *WSCL* 3(1962): 35–48. (Includes O'Neill, Miller, and Williams.)

21 WALTON, Ivan H. "Eugene O'Neill and the Folklore of the Sea." *WF* 14(1955): 153–169.

22 WEIGAND, Charmion von. "The Quest of Eugene O'Neill." *New Theatre* 2(1935): 12–17, 30–32.

1   WEISSMAN, Philip. "Conscious and Unconscious Autobiographical Dramas of Eugene O'Neill." *Journal of the American Psychoanalytic Association* 5(1957): 432–460. (Important.)*

2   WHICHER, Stephen. "O'Neill's Long Journey." *Commonweal* 43(1956): 614–615. (Review of world premiere in Stockholm of *Long Day's Journey into Night*.)

3   WINTHER, Sophus K. *Eugene O'Neill: A Critical Study*. New York: Random, 1934. Reprinted by Russell & Russell, 1961.

4   WINTHER, Sophus K. "Eugene O'Neill—The Dreamer Confronts His Dream." *ArQ* 21(1965): 221–233. (*More Stately Mansions* as an insight to O'Neill's mind.)

5   WINTHER, Sophus K. "O'Neill's Tragic Themes: *Long Day's Journey Into Night*." *ArQ* 13(1957): 295–307.

6   WINTHER, Sophus K. "Strindberg and O'Neill: A Study of Influence." *SS* 31(1959): 103–120.

7   WOODBRIDGE, Homer E. "Eugene O'Neill." *SAQ* 37(1938): 22–35.

8   YOUNG, Stark. "Eugene O'Neill: Notes from a Critic's Diary." *Harper's* 214(1957): 66–71, 74.

9   YOUNG, Stark. "O'Neill's Play, 'Mourning Becomes Electra'." *New Republic* 68(1931): 352–355.

10   YOUNG, Stark. See 13.14.

Rice, Elmer (1892–1967)

11   RICE, Elmer. *Seven Plays*. New York: Viking, 1950.

12   BROUSSARD, Louis. "Elmer Rice." See 20.2.

13   COLLINS, Ralph L. "The Playwright and the Press: Elmer Rice and His Critics." *TA* 7(1948–1949): 35–58.

14   DUSENBURY, Winifred L. "Socioeconomic Forces." See 21.11.

15   ELWOOD, William R. "An Interview with Elmer Rice on Expressionism." *ETJ* 20(1968): 1–7.

16   GASSNER, John. "Elmer Rice." See 14.10.

17   GOULD, Jean. "Elmer Rice." See 14.13.

18   HAMILTON, Clayton. "Elmer Rice." See 12.17.

19   HOGAN, Robert. *The Independence of Elmer Rice*. Carbondale, Ill.: Southern Illinois UP, 1965.

20   HUTCHENS, John. "Greece to Broadway." *TArts* 16(1932): 21–22.

21   JENNINGS, Richard. "Street Scene." *Spectator*, 145(1930): 407.

22   KRUTCH, Joseph W. "The Drama of Social Criticism." ·See 12.20.

23   KRUTCH, Joseph W. "The Prosecution Rests." *Nation* 136(1933): 158–160.

24   LEVIN, Meyer. "Elmer Rice." *TArts* 16(1932): 54–62.

25   LEWIS, Allan. "The Tired Deans—Elmer Rice and S. N. Behrman." See 14.18.

1   MANTLE, Burns. "Elmer Rice." See 13.2.

2   MANTLE, Burns. "Elmer Rice." See 13.1.

3   MERSAND, Joseph. "Elmer Rice: Realist of the Drama." See 13.3.

4   MOSES, Montrose J. "Elmer Rice." *Stage* 7(1930): 14–17.

5   MOSES, Montrose J. "Elmer Rice: A Dramatist Who Evokes Poetic Overtones Out of the City Streets." *Theatre Guild Mag* 7(1930): 15–17. 64.

6   NATHAN, George Jean. "Elmer Rice." See 15.5.

7   QUINN, Arthur H. "The New Decade, 1927–1936." See 6.3.

8   RABKIN, Gerald. "Elmer Rice and the Seriousness of Drama." See 8.15.

9   RICE, Elmer. " 'Author! Author!' or, How to Write a Smash Hit the First Time You Try." *AH* 16(1965): 46–49, 84–86.

10   RICE, Elmer. *Minority Report.* New York: Simon and Schuster, 1963.

11   RICE, Elmer. *The Living Theatre.* New York: Harper, 1959. (The practical aspects of the theatre as they relate to all concerned.)

12   SIEVERS, W. David. "Elmer Rice." See 8.9.

13   YOUNG, Stark. "Street Scene." *New Republic* 67(1929): 296–298.

Saroyan, William (1908–   )

14   BLOCK, Haskell, and Robert G. SHEDD. "William Saroyan." See 13.20.

15   BROWN, John Mason. "America's Yield." See 15.15.

16   BURGUM, Edwin B. "The Lonesome Young Man on the Flying Trapeze." *VQR* 20(1944): 392–403.

17   CARPENTER, Frederic I. "The Time of Saroyan's Life." *Pacific Spectator* 1(1947): 88–96. (Shows Saroyan in the tradition of Emerson and Whitman.)*

18   CHAPMAN, John. "Saroyan, Bless Him." *TArts* 42(1958): 25–26. (On *The Cave Dwellers.*)

19   *Don't Go Away Mad and Other Plays.* New York: Harcourt, Brace, 1949.

20   DUSENBURY, Winifred L. "Conflict between the Material and the Spiritual." See 21.11.

21   FISHER, William J. "What Ever Happened to Saroyan?" *CE* 16(1955): 336–340. (Saroyan, baffled at failure of the American dream, unable to give it up.)

22   FLOAN, Howard R. "Saroyan and Cervantes' Knight." *Thought* 33(1958): 81–92.

23   FLOAN, Howard R. *William Saroyan.* New York: Twayne, 1966. (Concentrates on the plots of plays and critical reactions.)

24   GAGEY, Edmond M. See 12.13.

1 GASSNER, John. "Saroyan: *The Time of Your Life.*" See 14.10.

2 HATCHER, Harlan. "William Saroyan." *EJ* 28(1939): 169–177.

3 KHERDIAN, David. *A Bibliography of William Saroyan.* San Francisco: Roger Beacham, 1966. (Lists only the writings that have appeared in book form.)

4 LEWIS, Allan. "The Comic Vein and 'Courage for Survival'." See 14.18.

5 MERSAND, Joseph. "William Saroyan and the American Imagination." *Players Mag* 17(1941): 9.

6 NATHAN, George Jean. "Saroyan: Whirling Dervish of Fresno." *American Mercury* 51(1940): 303–308.

7 RAHV, Philip. "William Saroyan: A Minority Report." *American Mercury* 57(1943): 371–377.

8 REMENYI, Joseph. "William Saroyan: A Portrait." *CE* 6(1944): 92–100.

9 SAROYAN, William. *Here Comes There Goes You Know Who.* New York: Simon and Schuster, 1961.

10 SAROYAN, William. "The Time of My Life." *TArts* 39(1955): 22–24, 95. (The author recollects his prize winning play.)

11 SAROYAN, William. "Twenty Years of Writing." *Atlantic* 195(1955): 65–68.

12 SAROYAN, William. "Why Does a Writer Write?" *SatR* 44(1961): 24, 46–47.

13 SIEVERS, W. David. "Surrealism—Stein and Saroyan." See 8.9.

14 *Three Plays by William Saroyan.* New York: Harcourt, Brace, 1941.

15 WILSON, Edmund. "The Boys in the Back Room: William Saroyan." *New Republic* 103(1940): 697–698.

Sherwood, Robert E[mmet] (1896–1955)

16 ANDERSON, Maxwell. "Robert E. Sherwood [1896–1955]." *TArts* 40(1956): 26–27, 87. (An appreciation.)

17 BREIT, Harvey. "An Interview with Robert E. Sherwood." *NYTBR*, Feb. 13, 1949, p. 23.

18 BROUSSARD, Louis. "Everyman at Mid-Century: Robert E. Sherwood." See 20.2.

19 BROWN, John Mason. "Allegory and Mr. Sherwood." See 11.19.

20 BROWN, John Mason. "America's Yield." See 15.15.

21 BROWN, John M. "The World of Robert Sherwood." *Horizon* 4(1962): 4–9.

22 BROWN, John Mason. *The Worlds of Robert E. Sherwood: Mirror to His Times, 1896–1939.* New York: Harper & Row, 1965. (The first volume of a two-volume biography.)*

23 CAMPBELL, O. J. "Robert Sherwood and His Times." *CE* 4(1943): 275–280.

24 DUSENBURY, Winifred L. "The Lonely Hero." See 21.11.

1   GASSNER, John. "Playwright in Transition: Robert Emmet Sherwood, 1941." See 14.10.

2   GASSNER, John. "Robert Emmet Sherwood." *Atlantic* 158(1942): 26–33.

3   GOULD, Jean. "Robert Sherwood." See 14.13.

4   ISAACS, E. J. R. "Robert Sherwood." *TArts* 23(1939): 31–40. (Pertinent discussions of the early plays.)*

5   KRUTCH, Joseph W. "Comedy." See 12.20.

6   KRUTCH, Joseph W. "The Devil's Tunes." *Nation* 142(1936): 490–492. (Treats important ideas and skill of expression.)

7   MANTLE, Burns. "Robert Sherwood." See 13.2.

8   NARDIN, James. "The Plays of Robert E. Sherwood." *Chrysalis* 10(1957): 3–14.

9   QUINN, Arthur H. "The New Decade, 1927–1936." See 6.3.

10 SHERWOOD, Robert E. "Footnote to a Preface." *SRL* 32(1949): 130, 132, 134.

11 SHUMAN, R. Baird. *Robert E. Sherwood.* New York: Twayne, 1964.

12 SIEVERS, W. David. "Robert Sherwood." See 8.9.

Wilder, Thornton (1897–   )

13 *The Angel That Troubled the Waters and Other Plays by Thornton Wilder.* New York: Coward McCann, 1928.

14 *The Long Christmas Dinner and Other Plays in One Act by Thornton Wilder.* New York: Coward McCann, 1931.

15 *Three Plays by Thornton Wilder.* New York: Harper, 1957.

16 ADCOCK, St. John. "Thornton Wilder." *Bookman* 69(1929): 316–319.

17 ADLER, Henry. "Thornton Wilder's Theatre." *Horizon* 12(1945): 89–98.

18 ARNAVON, Cyrille. "La Vogue de Thornton Wilder." *EA* 10(1957): 421–430.

19 BALLET, Arthur H. "In Our Living and in Our Dying." *EJ* 45(1956): 243–249. (On *Our Town*.)

20 BLOCK, Haskell, and Robert G. SHEDD. "Thornton Wilder." See 13.20.

21 BROUSSARD, Louis. "Thornton Wilder." See 20.2.

22 BROWN, E. K. "A Christian Humanist: Thornton Wilder." *UTQ* 4(1935): 356–370.

23 BROWN, John Mason. "Wilder: 'Our Town'." *SRL* 32(1949): 33–34.

24 BURBANK, Rex. *Thornton Wilder.* New York: Twayne, 1961. (A basic study.)

25 CAMPBELL, Joseph, and H. M. ROBINSON. "The Skin of Whose Teeth? The Strange Case of Mr. Wilder's New Play and 'Finnegan's Wake'." *SRL* 25(1942): 3–4; (1943): 16, 18–19.

1 CHAMBRUN, Longworth. "L'Américanisme de Thornton Wilder." *Revue Anglo-Américaine* 8(1931); 341–344.

2 CORRIGAN, Robert W. "Thornton Wilder and the Tragic Sense of Life." *ETJ* 13(1961): 161–173.

3 DELPECH, Janine. "Thornton Wilder." *NL* 30(1951); 1, 6.

4 EDELSTEIN, J. M. *A Bibliographical Checklist of the Writings of Thornton Wilder.* New Haven, Conn.: Yale U Library, 1959.*

5 FIREBAUGH, Joseph J. "The Humanism of Thornton Wilder." *Pacific Spectator* 4(1950): 426–438.

6 FRENZ, Horst. "The Reception of Thornton Wilder's Plays in Germany." *MD* 3(1960): 123–137.

7 FULLER, Edmund. "Thornton Wilder: The Notation of a Heart." *ASch* 28(1959): 210–217.

8 FUSSELL, Paul, Jr. "Thornton Wilder and the German Psyche." *Nation* 186(1958): 394–395.

9 GAGEY, Edmond M. "Poetry and Imagination." See 12.13.

10 GOLD, Michael. "Wilder: Prophet of the Genteel Christ." *New Republic* 61(1930): 266–267.

11 GOLDSTEIN, Malcolm. *The Art of Thornton Wilder.* Lincoln: U of Nebraska P, 1965. (A sound critical treatment.)

12 GOULD, Jean. "Thornton Wilder." See 14.13.

13 GREBANIER, Bernard. *Thornton Wilder.* U of Minnesota Pamphlets, No. 34. Minneapolis: U of Minnesota P, 1964. (Helpful introduction.)

14 GREENE, George. "The World of Thornton Wilder." *Thought* 37(1962): 563–584.

15 HABERMAN, Donald. *The Plays of Thornton Wilder: A Critical Study.* Middletown: Conn.: Wesleyan UP, 1967. (A thorough treatment.)*

16 HEWITT, Barnard. "Thornton Wilder Says 'Yes'." *TDR* 4(1959): 110–120.

17 ISAACS, E. J. R. "Thornton Wilder in Person." *TArts* 27(1943), 21–30.

18 KOHLER, Dayton. "Thornton Wilder." *EJ* 28(1939): 1–11.

19 KOSOK, Heinz. "Thornton Wilder: A Bibliography of Criticism." *TCL* 9(1963): 93–100.

20 LEWIS, Allan. "The Comic Vein and 'Courage for Survival'." See 14.18.

21 PAPAJEWSKI, Helmut. *Thornton Wilder.* Frankfurt Am Main: Athenäum Verlag, 1961. (A German analysis placing Wilder in relation to the Western European past.)

22 PARMENTER, Ross. "Novelist and Playwright." *SRL* 18(1938): 10–11.

23 ROBINSON, Henry M. "The Curious Case of Thornton Wilder." *Esquire* 47(1957): 70–71, 124–126.

24 SCOTT, Winfield. "*Our Town* and the Golden Veil." *VQR* 29(1953): 103–117. (Stresses integration of region and characters, typically imagined.)

1 SIEVERS, W. David. "Thornton Wilder." See 8.9.

2 STEPHENS, George D. *"Our Town*—Great American Tragedy?" *MD* 1(1959): 258–264.

3 TRITSCH, Walther. "Thornton Wilder in Berlin." *Living Age* 341(1931): 44–47.

4 VITTORINI, Elio. "Teatro Americano in Italia." *Galleria* (Italy) 4(1954); 302–306. (Discussion of *Our Town.*)

5 WILSON, Edmund. "The Antrobuses and the Earwickers." *Nation* 156(1943): 167–168.

6 WILSON, Edmund. "Thornton Wilder." *New Republic* 55(1928); 303–305.

Williams, Tennessee (Thomas Lanier) (1914–   )

7 *American Blues: Five Short Plays by Tennessee Williams.* New York: Dramatists Play Service, 1948.

8 ASSELINEAU, Roger. "Tennessee Williams ou la Nostalgie de la Purete." *EA* 10(1957): 431–443. (A critical survey of Williams' plays.)

9 ATKINSON, Brooks. "His Bizarre Images Can't Be Denied." *NYTBR* Nov. 26, 1961, pp. 1, 36.

10 BARKSDALE, Richard K. "Social Backgrounds in the Plays of Miller and Williams." See 36.15.

11 BLOCK, Haskell, and Robert G. SHEDD. "Tennessee Williams." See 13.20.

12 BLUEFARB, Sam. "The Glass Menagerie: Three Visions of Time." *CE* 24(1963); 513–518.

13 BROOKING, Jack. "Directing *Summer and Smoke:* An Existentialist Approach." *MD* 2(1960): 377–385.

14 BROOKS, Charles. "The Comic Tennessee Williams." *QJS* 44(1958): 275–281.

15 BROUSSARD, Louis. "Tennessee Williams." See 20.2.

16 BROWN, Andreas. "Tennessee Williams by Another Name." *PBSA* 57(1963): 377–378. (Locates eleven early pieces under the real name of Thomas L. Williams.)

17 BRUSTEIN, Robert. "Williams' Nebulous Nightmare." *HudR* 12(1959): 255–260. (Analysis of *Sweet Bird of Youth.*)

18 CALLAHAN, Edward F. "Tennessee Williams' Two Worlds." *NDQ* 25(1957): 61–67. (An analysis of Williams' plays to 1951.)

19 CARPENTER, Charles A., Jr., and Elizabeth COOK. "Addenda to 'Tennessee Williams, A Selected Bibliography'." *MD* 2(1959): 220–223.

20 CLURMAN, Harold. "Theatre Man with a Problem." *New Republic* 119(1948); 25–26.

21 DONY, Nadine. "Tennessee Williams: A Selected Bibliography." *MD* 1(1958): 181–191.

1 DUKORE, Bernard F. "American Abelard: A Footnote to *Sweet Bird of Youth*." *CE* 26(1965): 630–634.

2 DUKORE, Bernard F. "The Cat Has Nine Lives." *TDR* 8(1963): 95–100.

3 DUPNEY, Richard. "Tennessee Williams' Search for Innocence." *CathW* 189(1959): 191–194. (On *Sweet Bird of Youth*.)

4 DUSENBURY, Winifred L. "In the South." See 21.11.

5 ENCK, John J. "Memory and Desire and Tennessee Williams' Plays." *WASAL* 42(1953): 249–256.

6 FALK Signi Lenea. *Tennessee Williams*. New York: Twayne 1961. (Good study of Williams' literary qualities.)*

7 FEDDER, Norman J. *The Influence of D. H. Lawrence on Tennessee Williams*. The Hague: Mouton, 1966.

8 FREEMAN, Lucy. *Remember Me to Tom*. (As related by Edwina Dakin Williams.) New York: Putnam, 1963.

9 FUNKE, Lewis, and John E. BOOTH. "Williams on Williams." *TArts* 46(1962): 17–19, 72–73. (An interesting interview.)

10 GANZ, Arthur. "The Desperate Morality of the Plays of Tennessee Williams." *ASch* 31(1962): 278, 280, 282, 284, 286, 288, 290, 292, 294.

11 GASSNER, John. "The Influence of Strindberg in the United States." See 43.15.

12 GASSNER, John. "A Streetcar Named Desire: A Study in Ambiguity." See 14.10.

13 GASSNER, John. "Tennessee Williams: Dramatist of Frustation." *CE* 10(Oct., 1948): 1–7.

14 GASSNER, John. "Tennessee Williams: 1940–60." See 14.9.*

15 GIBBS, Wolcott. "The Brighter Side of Tennessee." *NY* 26(1951): 58–60.

16 GIBBS, Wolcott. "The Theatre Lower Depths, Southern Style." *NY*, 23(1947), 50–54.*

17 GOULD, Jean. "Tennessee Williams." See 14.13.

18 HEILMAN, Robert. "Tennessee Williams: Approaches to Tragedy." *SoR* 1(1965): 770–790.

19 HURT, James R. "*Suddenly Last Summer:* Williams and Melville. *MD* 3(1961): 396–400.

20 JACKSON, Esther M. *The Broken World of Tennessee Williams*. Madison: U of Wisconsin P, 1965. (A competent critical appraisal.)*

21 JACKSON, Esther M. "The Problem of Form in the Drama of Tennessee Williams." *CLAJ* 4(1960): 8–12.

22 JONES, Robert E. "Tennessee Williams' Early Heroines." *MD* 2(1959): 211–219.

23 KERNAN, Alvin B. "Truth and Dramatic Mode in the Modern Theater: Chekhov, Pirandello, and Williams." *MD* 1(1958): 101–114. (Discusses *A Streetcar Named Desire*.)

24 KERR, Walter. "The Rose Tattoo." *Commonweal* 53(1951): 492–494.

1 LEE, M. Owen. "Orpheus and Eurydice: Some Modern Versions." *CJ* 56(1961): 307–313.

2 LEWIS, Allan. "Tennessee Williams—The Freedom of the Senses." See 14.18.

3 MAXWELL, Gilbert. *Tennessee Williams and Friends.* Cleveland: World, 1965.

4 MOOR, Paul. "A Mississippian Named Tennessee." *Harper's* 197(1948): 63–71.

5 NATHAN, George Jean. "Tennessee Williams." See 15.5.

6 NELSON, Benjamin. *Tennessee Williams: The Man and His Work.* New York: Ivan Obolensky, 1961. (Penetrating study of the mixture of genius and banality in Williams.)*

7 POPKIN, Henry. "The Plays of Tennessee Williams." *TDR* 4(1960): 45–64.

8 REBONA, Roberto. "Estate fumo di Tennessee Williams. Ritagli crepuscolari decadenti." *La Fiera Letteraria* 63(1950): 8.

9 ROSS, Don. "Williams in Art and Morals." New York *Herald Tribune*, March 3, 1957, Section 4, pp. 1, 2.

10 SHARP, William. "An Unfashionable View of Tennessee Williams." *TDR* 6(1962): 160–171.

11 SIEVERS, W. David. "Tennessee Williams and Arthur Miller." See 8.9.

12 STAVRON, Constantine N. "The Neurotic Heroine in Tennessee Williams." *Literature & Psychology* 5(1955): 26–34.

13 TAYLOR, Harry. "The Dilemma of Tennessee Williams." *Masses and Mainstream* 1(1948): 51–56.

14 *Three Plays by Tennessee Williams.* New York: New Directions, 1948.

15 TISCHLER, Nancy M. *Tennessee Williams: Rebellious Puritan.* New York: Citadel, 1961. (Views Williams as a neoromantic; detailed account of his early years.)*

16 *27 Wagon Loads of Cotton and Other One-Act Plays.* New York: New Directions, 1945.

17 TYNAN, Kenneth. "American Blues: The Plays of Arthur Miller and Tennessee Williams." See 38.22.

18 VOWLES, Richard B. "Psychology and Drama: A Selected Checklist." See 46.20.

19 VOWLES, Richard B. "Tennessee Williams: The World of His Imagery." *TDR* 3(1958): 51–56.

20 WATERS, Arthur B. "Tennessee Williams: Ten Years Later." *TArts* 39(1955): 72–73, 96. (Chiefly on *Cat on a Hot Tin Roof.*)

21 WEALES, Gerald. "Tennessee Williams' *Fugitive Kind.*" See 10.5.

22 WEALES, Gerald. *Tennessee Williams.* U of Minnesota Pamphlets, No. 53. Minneapolis: U of Minnesota P, 1965. (Brief but penetrating.)*

23 WEISSMAN, Philip. "Psychological Characters in Current Drama." *AI* 17(1960): 271–278. (Psychoanalytic study of *A Streetcar Named Desire.*)

1 WILLIAMS, Edwina D., and Lucy FREEMAN. "Remember Me to Tom." *Show* 3(1963): 60–61, 103–105. (Reminiscences by Williams' mother.)

2 WOODS, John. "Tennessee Williams as a Poet." *Poetry* 90(1957): 256–258.

3 YARNGH, Vernon. "Social Drama and Big Daddy." *SWR* 41(Spring, 1956): 194–197. (Compares Williams' characters unfavorably with Chekhov's.)

Lesser American Dramatists

Ade, George (1866–1944)

4 BAUERLE, Richard F. "A Look at the Language of George Ade." *AS* 33(1958): 77–79.

5 BROOKS, Van Wyck. "Chicago: Four Writers." *The Confident Years* See 1.10.

6 COYLE, Lee. *George Ade*. New York: Twayne, 1964. (Biographical with sketches of plots.)

7 DICKINSON, Thomas H. "The 'Little Man' as Dramatic Hero: George Ade." See 12.8.

8 KELLY, Fred C. *George Ade: Warmhearted Satirist*. Indianapolis: Bobbs-Merrill, 1947.

9 MENCKEN, H. L. "George Ade." *Prejudices: First Series*. New York: Knopf, 1919.

10 MOSES, Montrose J. "George Ade." See 6.1.

11 QUINN, Arthur H. "Comedy Types Again." See 6.3.

12 RUSSO, Dorothy R. *A Bibliography of George Ade, 1866–1944*. Indianapolis: Indiana Historical Society, 1947.

Barker, James Nelson (1784–1858)

13 DUNLAP, William. See 10.10.

14 EARNHART, Phyllis H. "The First American Play in England." *AL* 31(1959): 326–329. (Questions Barker's authorship of *Pocahontas*.)

15 MUSSER, Paul H. *James Nelson Barker, 1784–1858*. Philadelphia: U of Pennsylvania P, 1929. (Factual study with special attention to sources, and a full bibliography of primary and secondary material.)*

16 QUINN, Arthur H. "James Nelson Barker and the Native Plays, 1805–1825." See 6.2.

Belasco, David (1859–1931)

1 BELASCO, David. *The Theatre through Its Stage Door.* New York: Harper, 1919. (Recounts many of Belasco's productions.)*

2 BROWN, John Mason. "David Belasco." See 12.1.

3 EATON, Walter P. "David Belasco." See 12.11.

4 *The Heart of Maryland and Other Plays* by David Belasco. Ed. by Glenn Hughes and George Savage. Princeton, N.J.: Princeton UP, 1941.

5 MANTLE, Burns. "David Belasco." See 13.1.

6 MOSES, Montrose J. "David Belasco and the Psychology of the Switchboard." See 6.1.

7 MOSES, Montrose J. "David Belasco: The Astonishing Versatility of a Veteran Producer." *Theatre Guild Magazine* 7(1929): 27–30, 51.

8 *The Plays of Henry C. De Mille*, written in collaboration with David Belasco. Ed. by Robert H. Ball. Princeton, N.J.: Princeton UP, 1941.

9 QUINN, Arthur H. "David Belasco and His Associates." See 6.3.

10 SIEVERS, W. David. "David Belasco Discovers Sex." See 8.9.

11 TIMBERLAKE, Craig. *The Bishop of Broadway: The Life and Work of David Belasco.* New York: Library Pub, 1954.

12 WINTER, William. *The Life of David Belasco.* 2 vols. New York: Moffat, Yard, 1918.*

13 YOUNG, Stark. "Estimate of David Belasco." *New Republic* 47(1931): 123–124.

Bird, Robert Montgomery (1806–1854)

14 *The Cowled Lover & Other Plays* by Robert Montgomery Bird. Ed. by Edward H. O'Neill. Princeton, N.J.: Princeton UP, 1941.

15 DAHL, Curtis. *Robert Montgomery Bird.* New York: Twayne, 1963. (Well-documented biography and comprehensive analysis of the plays.)*

16 FOUST, Clement E. *The Life and Dramatic Works of Robert Montgomery Bird.* New York: Knickerbocker, 1919. (Documented and authoritative. Biography and collection of four plays.)*

17 HARRIS, Richard. "From the Papers of R. M. Bird: the Lost Scene from *News of the Night*." *LCUP* 24(1958): 1–12.

18 HARRIS, Richard, ed. "A Young Dramatist's Diary: The Secret Records of R. M. Bird." *LCUP* 25(Winter, 1959): 8–24. (Discussion and text of *The Secret Records*.)

19 QUINN, Arthur H. "Robert Montgomery Bird and the Rise of the Romantic Play, 1825–1850." See 6.2.

20 THOMPSON, C. S. "Life of Robert Montgomery Bird: Written by His Wife, Mary Mayer Bird . . . with Selections from Bird's Correspondence." *U Penn Lib Chron* 12(1944), 71–120: 13(1945): 1–94.

Boucicault, Dion (1820–1890)

1   ENKVIST, Nils E. "*The Octoroon* and English Opinions of Slavery." *AQ* 8(1956): 166–170. (English sympathy for the Confederacy caused Boucicault to substitute a happy ending.)

2   FAULKNER, Seldon. "The *Octoroon* War." *ETJ* 15(1963): 33–38.

3   *Forbidden Fruit and Other Plays* by Dion Boucicault. Ed. by Allardyce Nicoll and F. Theodore Cloak. Princeton, N.J.: Princeton UP, 1940.

4   GAMBONE, Kenneth. "Boucicault's Contributions to Theatre." *Ball State Teachers Coll Forum* 4(1963): 73–78.

5   JEFFERSON, Joseph. See 7.4.

6   KAPLAN, Sidney. "*The Octoroon*: Early History of the Drama of Miscegenation." *Journal of Negro Education* 20(1951): 547–557.

7   MOSES, Montrose J. "The Prolific Dion Boucicault." See 6.1.

8   QUINN, Arthur H. "The Influence of Dion Boucicault." See 6.2.

9   RAHILL, Frank. "Dion Boucicault." *TArts* 23(1939): 807–813.

10   WALLACK, Lester. See 7.15.

11   WALSH, Townsend. *The Career of Dion Boucicault.* New York: Dunlap Society, 1915.

Cohan, George M. (1878–1942)

12   COHAN, George M. *Twenty Years on Broadway and the Years It Took to Get There.* New York: Harper, 1925.*

13   DICKINSON, Thomas H. "George M. Cohan." See 12.8.

14   MOSES, Montrose J. "Forms of American Drama." See 6.1.

15   QUINN, Arthur H. "Comedy Types Again." See 6.3.

Daly, Augustin (1838–1899)

16   DALY, Joseph F. *Life of Augustin Daly.* New York: Macmillan, 1917.

17   FELHEIM, Marvin. *The Theater of Augustin Daly: An Account of the Late Nineteenth Century American Stage.* Cambridge: Harvard UP, 1956.*

18   *Man and Wife & Other Plays* by Augustin Daly. Ed. by Catherine Sturtevant. Princeton, N.J.: Princeton UP, 1942.

19   MOSES, Montrose J. "An Unaccented Phase of Augustin Daly." See 6.1.

20   QUINN, Arthur H. "Augustin Daly, Constructive Artist of the Theatre." See 6.3.

21   SKINNER, Cornelia Otis. "Daly's." See 7.12.

1 SKINNER, Otis. See 7.13.

Davis, Owen (1874–1956)

2 DAVIS, Owen. *I'd Like to Do It Again.* New York: Farrar, Rinehart, 1931. (Autobiography.)

3 DAVIS, Owen. *My First Fifty Years in the Theatre.* Boston: Walter H. Baker, 1950. (Informal view of the theatre from 1897 to 1947 by a playwright.)

4 GAGEY, Edmond M. See 12.13.

5 MANTLE, Burns. "Owen Davis." See 13.1.

6 MANTLE, Burns. "Owen Davis." See 13.2.

7 MOSES, Montrose J. "Owen Davis: The Infallible Playwright Whose Gamut Extends from the Thriller to a Pulitzer Prize Play." *Theatre Guild Magazine* 8(1930): 42–44.

8 QUINN, Arthur H. "The New Realism of Character." See 6.3.

9 SIEVERS, W. David. "Owen Davis." See 8.9.

Dunlap, William (1766–1839)

10 *False Shame and Thirty Years* by William Dunlap. Ed. by Oral S. Coad. Princeton, N.J.: Princeton UP, 1940.

11 BENSON, Adolph B. "Scandinavian Influences in the Works of William Dunlap and Richard Alsop." *SS* 9(1927): 239–257.

12 BOWMAN, M. R. "Dunlap and the 'Theatrical Register' of the *New York Magazine*." *SP* 24(1927): 413–425.

13 BROOKS, Van Wyck. "William Dunlap and His Circle." *The World of Washington Irving.* See 1.10.

14 CANARY, Robert H. "William Dunlap and the Search for an American Audience." *Midcontinent American Studies Journal*, 4(1963), 45–51.

15 COAD, Oral S. "The Dunlap Diaries at Yale." *SP* 24(1927): 403–412.

16 COAD, Oral S. "The Gothic Element in American Literature Before 1835." *JEGP* 24(1925): 72–93.

17 COAD, Oral S. *William Dunlap: A Study of His Life and Works and of His Place in Contemporary Culture.* New York: Russell & Russell, 1962. (First published in 1917 by the Dunlap Society.)*

18 COAD, Oral S. "William Dunlap: New Jersey Artist." *NJHSP* 83(1965): 238–263.

19 GREEN, David Bonnell. "Letters of William Godwin and Thomas Holcroft to William Dunlap." *N&Q* 3(1956): 441–443.

20 MATLAW, Myron. "*Menschenhass und Reue* in *English*." *Sym* 14(1960): 129–134. (Account of a version of Kotzebue's drama by William Dunlap.)

1 MORAMARCO, Fred. "The Early Dramatic Criticism of William Dunlap." *AL* 40(1968): 9–14.

2 MOSES, Montrose J. "William Dunlap and His Contemporaries." See 6.1.

3 QUINN, Arthur H. "William Dunlap, Playwright and Producer." See 6.2.

4 WYLD, Lionel D. "A Farce on Erie Water." *NYFQ* 17(1961): 59–62. (Treats Dunlap's *A Trip to Niagara*.)

Gillette, William (1855–1937)

5 MOSES, Montrose J. "William Gillette." See 6.1.

6 QUINN, Arthur H. "William Gillette and the Realism of Action." See 6.3.

7 STONE, P. M. "Mr. William Gillette." *Sherlock Holmes Jour* 4(1960): 115–118. (Discusses Gillette's *Sherlock Holmes*.)

Glaspell, Susan (1882–1948)

8 DICKINSON, Thomas H. "Susan Glaspell." See 12.8.

9 GLASPELL, Susan. *The Road to the Temple, the Life of George Cram Cook*. New York: Stokes, 1927. (Biography of her husband.)

10 GOULD, Jean. "Susan Glaspell and the Provincetown Players." See 14.13.

11 QUINN, Arthur H. "The New Realism of Character." See 6.3.

12 SIEVERS, W. David. "Susan Glaspell and George Cram Cook." See 8.9.

13 WATERMAN, Arthur E. *Susan Glaspell*. New York: Twayne, 1966.

Godfrey, Thomas (1736–1763)

14 CARLSON, C. L. "Thomas Godfrey in England." *AL* 7(1935): 302–309.

15 CARLSON, C. L. "A Further Note on Thomas Godfrey in England." *AL* 9(1937): 73–77.

16 GEGENHEIMER, Albert F. "Thomas Godfrey: Protege of William Smith." *Pennsylvania History* 9(1942): 233–251; 10(1943): 26–43.

17 GEORGE, Dorothy. "More Evidence on an Early Theatrical Withdrawal." *Am. N&Q* 2(1942): 100–101.

18 MOSES, Montrose J. "Our Colonial Theatre." See 6.1.

19 POLLOCK, T. C. "Rowe's *Tamerlane* and *The Prince of Parthia*." *AL* 6(1934): 158–162.

20 QUINN, Arthur H. "The Drama and the Theatre in the Colonies." See 6.2.

1   SEILHAMER, George O. Vol. I, pp. 185–195. See 11.3.

2   TYLER, Moses Coit. Vol. II, pp. 244–251. See 11.4.

Harrigan, Edward (1845–1911)

3   KAHN, E. J., Jr. "Profiles." *NY*3 1(March 19, 1955): 42–64; (March 26, 1955): 39–65; (April 2, 1955): 45–63; (April 9, 1955); 41–75. (Edward Harrigan, Tony Hart, and the New York Irish theatre of post-Civil War era.)

4   MOSES, Montrose J. "Edward Harrigan and Charles Hoyt." See 6.1.

5   QUINN, Arthur H. "Harrigan, Hoyt, and the Comedy of Types." See 6.3.

Hart, Moss (1904–1961)

6   GILDER, Rosamund. "The Fabulous Hart." *TArts* 28(1944): 89–98.

7   GOULD, Jean. "George S. Kaufman and Moss Hart." See 14.13.

8   HART, Moss. See 35.8.

9   KAPLAN, Charles. "Two Depression Plays and Broadway's Popular Idealism." *AQ* 15(1963): 579–585. (Treats Odet's *Awake and Sing* and Kaufman and Hart's *You Can't Take It With You*.)

10   MANTLE, Burns. "Moss Hart." See 13.2.

11   NATHAN, George Jean. "Moss Hart." See 15.5.

12   SIEVERS, W. David. "Moss Hart." See 8.9.

Howard, Bronson (1842–1908)

13   *The Banker's Daughter & Other Plays* by Bronson Howard. Ed. by Allan G. Halline. Princeton, N.J.: Princeton UP, 1941.

14   HALLINE, Allan, G. "Bronson Howard's *The Amateur Benefit*." *AL* 14(1942): 74–76.

15   MARSHALL, Thomas J. "Performances of Bronson Howard's *The Amateur Benefit*." *AL* 14(1942): 311–312.

16   MOSES, Montrose J. "Bronson Howard: Dean of the American Drama." See 6.1.

17   QUINN, Arthur H. "Bronson Howard and the Establishment of Professional Playwrighting." See 6.3.

Hoyt, Charles Hale (1860–1900)

18   *Five Plays* by Charles H. Hoyt. Ed. by Douglas L. Hunt. Princeton, N.J.: Princeton UP, 1941.

1 HAPGOOD, Norman. "Charles H. Hoyt." See 11.8.

2 HORNBLOW, Arthur. See 6.7.

3 MOSES, Montrose J. "Edward Harrigan and Charles Hoyt." See 6.1.

4 QUINN, Arthur H. "Harrigan, Hoyt, and the Comedy of Types." See 6.3.

Kelly, George (1887–   )

5 BROWN, John Mason. "The Playwright and the American Theatre." See 12.1.

6 DICKINSON, Thomas H. "Modern Domestic Comedy: George Kelly." See 12.8.

7 DOYLE, Paul A. "George Kelly: An Eclectic Bibliography." *BB* 24(1965): 173–174, 177.

8 DUSENBURY, Winifred L. "Conflict between the Material and the Spiritual." See 21.11.

9 KRUTCH, Joseph W. "Three New Realists." See 12.20.

10 MANTLE, Burns. "George Kelly." See 13.1.

11 MANTLE, Burns. "George Kelly." See 13.2.

12 MOSES, Montrose J. *Dramas of Modernism and Their Forerunners.* Boston: Little, Brown, 1941.

13 MOSES, Montrose J. "George Kelly: His Satire Stings Our Middle Class and Especially Its Women." *Theatre Guild Magazine* 7(1930): 14–17.

14 QUINN, Arthur H. "The New Realism of Character." See 6.3.

15 SIEVERS, W. David. "George Kelly." See 8.9.

MacKaye, Percy (1875–1956)

16 *Poems and Plays* by Percy MacKaye. 2 vols. New York: Macmillan, 1916.

17 BOTKIN, B. A. "Folk Speech in the Kentucky Mountain Cycle of Percy MacKaye." *AS* 6(1931): 267–276.

18 CLARK, Barrett H. See 12.5.

19 CROWLEY, Allister. "Percy MacKaye." *International* 11(1917): 47.

20 DICKINSON, Thomas H. "The Playwright as Pioneer: Percy MacKaye." See 12.8.

21 EATON, Walter P. See 12.11.

22 MOSES, Montrose J. "The Case of Percy MacKaye and His Father." See 6.1.

23 QUINN, Arthur H. "Percy MacKaye and the Drama as Spectacle." See 6.3.

MacKaye, Steele (1842–1894)

1 *An Arrant Knave & Other Plays* by Steele MacKaye. Ed. by Percy MacKaye. Princeton, N.J.: Princeton UP, 1941.

2 MAC KAYE, Percy. *Epoch: The Life of Steele MacKaye.* 2 vols. New York: Liveright, 1927. (Authoritative biography and a good account of the theatre of the period.)*

3 MOSES, Montrose J. "The Case of Percy MacKaye and His Father." See 6.1.

4 QUINN, Arthur H. "Realism of Character." See 6.3.

Mowatt, Anna Cora (1819–1870)

5 BARNES, Erich. *The Lady of Fashion: Anna Cora Mowatt.* New York: Scribner's, 1954.

6 MOSES, Montrose J. "American Dramatists and Their Infant Industry." See 6.1.

7 MOWATT, Anna Cora. *The Autobiography of an Actress.* Boston: Ticknor, Reed, and Fields, 1854.

8 QUINN, Arthur H. "American Comedy Types, 1825–1860." See 6.2.

Payne, John Howard (1791–1852)

9 *The Last Duel in Spain & Other Plays* by John Howard Payne. Ed. by Codman Hislop and W. R. Richardson. Princeton, N.J.: Princeton UP, 1940.

10 *Trial Without Jury & Other Plays* by John Howard Payne. Ed. by Codman Hislop and W. R. Richardson. Princeton , N.J.: Princeton UP, 1940.

11 BOULTER, E. Merton. "John Howard Payne's Visit to Georgia." *GHQ* 46(1962): 333–376.

12 BROOKS, Van Wyck. "Washington Irving in England." *The World of Washington Irving.* See 1.10.

13 DE BAILLOU, Clemens. *John Howard Payne to His Countrymen.* Athens: U of Georgia P, 1961.

14 FOREMAN, Grant. "John Howard Payne and the Cherokee Indians." *Am Hist Rev* 37(1932): 723–750.

15 GILBERT, Morris. "The Stage Career of John Howard Payne." *NOQ* 23(1950–1951): 59–74.

16 HARRISON, Gabriel. *John Howard Payne.* Philadelphia: Lippincott, 1885.

17 HEARTMAN, C. F., and H. B. WEISS. "John Howard Payne: A Bibliography." *ABC* 3(Jan., March, April, May–June, 1933): 55–57, 181–184, 224–228, 305–307; 4(July, Aug., 1933): 27–29, 78–82.

18 LEARY, Lewis, and Arlin TURNER. "John Howard Payne in New Orleans." *La Hist Quart,* 31(1948): 110–122. (Biographical.)

19 LUQUER, Thatcher T. Payne. "Correspondence of Washington Irving and John Howard Payne." *Scribner's* 48(1910): 461–482, 597–616.

20 MORRIS, Muriel. "Mary Shelley and John Howard Payne." *London Mercury* 22(1930): 443–450.

1   MOSES, Montrose J. "John Howard Payne." See 6.1.

2   OVERMYER, Grace. *America's First Hamlet*. New York: New York UP, 1957. (A biography of John Howard Payne.)

3   OVERMYER, Grace. "The Baltimore Mobs and John Howard Payne." *MHM* 58(1963): 54–61.

4   QUINN, Arthur H. "John Howard Payne and the Foreign Plays, 1805–1825." See 6.2.

5   WILKINS, Thurman. "John Howard Payne: Friend of the Cherokees." *CLC* 12(1962): 3–11.

Riggs, Lynn (1899–1954)

6   CAMPBELL, W. S. "Lynn Riggs: Poet and Dramatist." *SWR* 15(1929): 64–70.

7   GAGEY, Edmond M. See 12.13.

8   QUINN, Arthur H. "The New Decade, 1927–1936." See 6.3.

9   SIEVERS, W. David. "Western Freudians: Totheroh and Riggs." See 8.9.

Sheldon, Edward (1886–1946)

10 BARNES, Eric W. *The Man Who Lived Twice: The Biography of Edward Sheldon*. New York: Scribner's, 1956.

11 CLARK, Barrett H. "Edward Sheldon." See 12.4.

12 DICKINSON, Thomas H. "Edward Sheldon." See 12.8.

13 DOWNER, Alan. "Toward Drama." See 12.9.

14 GAGEY, Edmond M. See 12.13.

15 QUINN, Arthur H. "Edward Sheldon, Playwright of Passion and Aspiration." See 6.3.

Thomas, Augustus (1857–1934)

16 BURTON, Richard. "Augustus Thomas." See 12.2.

17 CLARK, Barrett H. See 12.5.

18 EATON, Walter P. See 12.11.

19 MOSES, Montrose J. "The Story of the Well-Made Play." See 6.1.

20 QUINN, Arthur H. "Augustus Thomas and the Picture of American Life." See 6.3.

21 SIEVERS, W. David. "Augustus Thomas." See 8.9.

22 THOMAS, Augustus. *The Print of My Remembrance*. New York: Scribner's, 1922. (Thomas' introductions to his plays.)*

Tyler, Royall (1757–1826)

1 BROOKS, Van Wyck. "New England." *World of Washington Irving.* See 1.10.

2 *Four Plays* by Royall Tyler. Ed. by Arthur W. Peach and George F. New-brough. Princeton, N.J.: Princeton U Press, 1941.

3 KILLHEFFER, Marie. "A Comparison of the Dialect of the 'Bigelow Papers' with the Dialect of Four Yankee Plays." *AS* 3(1928): 222–236.

4 LAUBER, John. "*The Contrast:* A Study in the Concept of Innocence." *ELN* 1(1963): 33–37.

5 NETHERCOT, A. H. "The Dramatic Background of Royall Tyler's *The Contrast.*" *AL* 12(1941): 435–446.

6 NEWBROUGH, G. F. "Mary Tyler's Journal." *VtQ* 20(1952): 19–31. (A day-to-day journal of Royall Tyler's last days.)

7 QUINN, Arthur H. "The Coming of Comedy." See 6.2.

8 STEIN, Roger B. "Royall Tyler and the Question of Our Speech." *NEQ* 38(1965): 454–474.

9 TANSELLE, G. Thomas. *Royall Tyler.* Cambridge, Mass.: Harvard UP, 1967. (An excellent account of the man and his writing.)*

Walter, Eugene (1874–1941)

10 DICKINSON, Thomas H. "Eugene Walter." See 12.8.

11 DOWNER, Alan. See 12.9.

12 QUINN, Arthur H. "The Height of Melodrama." See 6.3.

13 WALTER, Eugene. *How to Write a Play.* New York: Eugene Walter, 1925. (Handbook for students.)

NOTES

INDEX

INDEX

INDEX H—K

INDEX